Timber Footbridges

Edgar (Ted) Stubbersfield

DEDICATION

This book is dedicated to Dr. Dan Tingley, a friend, an encouragement and a brother. I appreciate you and your wisdom and superior knowledge very much.

CONTENTS

Acknowledgments

Considerable time and effort was taken by the archivists in the Department of Transport and Main Roads to find information about two historical bridges I have included. Their help is much appreciated. As well I would like to acknowledge my good friends Dennis and Carole whose proofreading compensates for my dyslexia.

Background

My beginning as a bridge builder started in a very unlikely way back in 1984. I was asked by a concrete casting company that our family hardware store purchased paving squares from to price a timber footbridge built on log girders with sawn timber rails and decking. The price was for possible resale by them to their local government. I ran a few numbers and gave a price and, to my surprise, got the order to supply the bridge. I was surprised as I had added in a manufacturer's profit over and above the trade price of material and the reseller also had a profit.

We were in an ideal position to supply this bridge as my family were sawmillers, had a timber treatment plant for producing power poles, had cranes to handle the heavy girders and good contacts with builders. Up to that point, I had only been a supplier of timber and hardware and this was the first time I had actually built something. It was a great feeling but it was more than that. As the bridge quickly took shape, I realised that here was a product that suited the high quality, high durability timbers I had available and which, even more importantly, I could sell profitably. The plans were not copyright so I was away. All we had to do was ignore the timber specification (F14) and supply suitable timber. Soon after that bridge sale there followed a large order for traffic barriers and my sight was firmly set on moving away from general house framing. That was a market where no-one was prepared to pay the premium needed for good quality timber. I quickly learnt that a piece of timber had one price but, if I cut it to length and drilled a couple of holes in it and called it a product and did some marketing, it had a totally different price.

Fig. 1. My disastrous bridge!

This is a book that almost did not happen as my entry into the footbridge market was almost cut very short. Let me tell you a tale of woe with the hope that you will proceed with extreme caution. There was an old retired engineer in Gatton, where our business was situated, who did any drawings and

1

certification I needed for a very modest fee. I was asked if I could build a 20 metre clear span bridge and he told me that it was quite straightforward using a Barrup truss. He gave me some sketches sufficient to prepare a quotation and an order followed. I looked at the completed drawings and a very uneasy feeling came over me. I sent the plans off to another engineer to be checked and the reply came back, "Everything is in order". Still unsettled, I had another engineer check the rope design and again it was given the tick of approval. The bridge was duly loaded and shipped off. Soon after, the client rang to say the bridge was a disaster. The girders had turned into an "S". With an awfully sick feeling in my stomach I then rang Timber Queensland to see if there was a specialist timber engineer in Queensland who could advise me as the professional advice received and reality were not matching.

They recommended a consultant, James Pierce of James Pierce and Associates[1], and he looked at the design and came back and told me, "Of course the girders have become an "S". They could not do anything else." I had found a consultant who understood timber and, more importantly, I found a consultant I could trust and so started a relationship that lasted for over 20 years. I had the confidence to move forward with the assurance that I would not embarrass another client. As I wanted to get more involved in bridges I was fortunate to receive a grant which enabled me to engage Mr Pierce to research footbridges and write a report enabling me to learn what I needed to know to understand the product and authoritatively advise my clients. This report was published as the *Light Bridge Manual*. That book dealt with "What" had to be built whereas this book is primarily concerned with "How" to build it in timber.

If there was one disadvantage with our relationship it was that we found that our consultant's deep understanding of both timber and the bridge code often disadvantaged us when we were quoting against others. Invariably, purchasers looked only at price and not specification and performance. Maintenance costs were moved to another department.[2] Nonetheless, we still produced some remarkable footbridges in timber and in timber and steel.

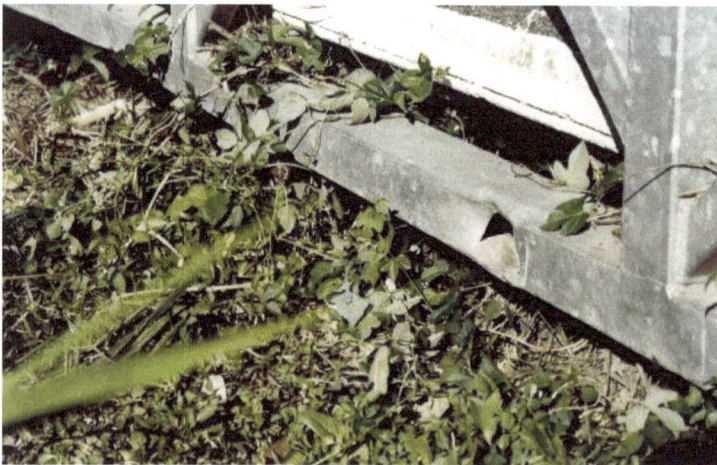

Fig. 2. Light steel in truss bottom chord damaged is by a council mover.

Fig. 3 Light steel bridge braced back to road bridge for stability.

Overall, I am somewhat pessimistic about the footbridge market (and the bridges in Figures Two and

---

[1] At the time of writing, Mr Pierce is retired.

[2] Whereas the steel in the truss bridge in Figure Two is so light the mower has bent the bottom chord and punctured the steel, our started at 100x4 SHS and our bridges had a minimum frequency of 5 Hertz or above meaning that extra bracing seen in Figure Three was not needed. Similar problems occur with timber bridges.

Three give good reason for this outlook). I am convinced that a rethink of the practice of purchasing on price is needed. Tragically, I can only see this happening after a high profile bridge collapse. Too often, specifiers and designers are working outside of their field of expertise and, while they may specify "Footbridge to AS5100", can't assess whether the bridge they receive really is suitable for their needs.

My frustrations experienced trying to sell trouble free, low maintenance bridges has prompted me to write this book so standards might be raised. This book is intended to assist the following:

Footbridge purchasers: Footbridges can and do fail and the best time asset owners have to address that risk is at the time of purchase. This book will, in part, give guidance to the asset owner on preparing the specification and so avoid shortcomings that have been seen in some kit bridges.

Professional designers: My intention is not to teach you how to engineer the structure. This book will allow you to take the skills you already have and allow you to recognise where extra care has to be taken. By detailing your bridges well, they will age gracefully and exceed your client's expectations. While there is little actual engineering in this book, just detailing, you can find span charts in my other publications:

- Boardwalk Design Guide
- Deckwood Selection Guide and
- Commercial Barrier Guide

To some extent, this book is my personal journey with footbridges and I recount the mistakes I have made and mistakes made by others. From these, you will see how logical timber design is and how easy it can be to design out the durability issues that can be associated with timber. This book will have been a success if purchasers become more discerning in their approach to footbridges in general and designers approach timber footbridges with confidence.

1. Why Timber Footbridges

Though the chapter is entitled, *Why Timber Footbridges* some might be asking, "Why ever would you use a timber footbridge?" I have a lot of sympathy with that question. Over my professional life I saw a move away from durable hardwoods to plantation pine for bridges and boardwalks by Queensland councils. This was driven by the need to be seen to be doing the right thing environmentally. However, it was done without understanding the implications of their choices. Councils adopted policies that rejected proven products in favour of timbers that had been rejected 200 years ago as unsuitable. Timber treatment could stop decay but could not prevent the pine behaving like pine. That is, self destructing from the effect of wetting and drying.

While pine was relatively successful in shaded areas for boardwalks (and in much cooler climates than my own in Queensland), it was a bitter disappointment in fully exposed areas which, invariably, footbridges are. I have seen many tenders for replacements of these pine bridges but never one where they have been replaced with timber. Fortunately, pine is now only infrequently being specified for boardwalks in my home state, though I still see it being used for bridges. The use of unsuitable species and construction methods have done immense harm to the timber footbridge industry.

Fig. 4 Pine truss damaged in flood about to be replaced.

Fig. 5. The replacement bridge in fibre composite and stainless steel.

Sadly, we find that reason goes out the window when it comes to timber bridges. Now, many people will not consider a timber bridge and, invariably, they will cite past experience. While a certain hesitation is understandable, it is not applied uniformly over competing materials. A badly designed bridge built with the wrong timbers and poor construction practices should be considered as just that, and not representative of the life they should expect. Timber should not be rejected out of hand just as a poorly designed steel or concrete structure should dissuade any designer from using these materials. To understand what is possible, consider the following examples.

In Europe, there are bridges that are hundreds of years old. Probably the most famous example is the Kapellbrücke (literally Chapel Bridge), a covered wooden footbridge across the Reuss River in Lucerne Switzerland. It dates back to 1333! The bridge was heavily damaged by fire in 1993 and rebuilt in timber. It is Europe's oldest covered bridge and oldest truss bridge. A number of bridges[3] built during the 16th century by the State of Berne are still in use. Most have their original main elements and some still carry heavy traffic.[4]

Fig. 6. Chapel Bridge, Lucerne, Switzerland.

---

[3] These being Neubrugg, 1532, Gummenen 1555, Wangen 1559, and Aarberg, 1568.
[4] Freedman, G, C. Mattem. P. Larsen, S. Edwards, T, Reynolds. *Timber Bridges and Foundations. A report produced for the Forestry Commission*, November 2002. No publication details.

The Sawmill Creek Bridge in Albert County, New Brunswick, Canada was a highway bridge built in 1905 and served in this capacity till 1975 when it was replaced with a new concrete bridge. The historical bridge was relocated nearby and now serves as a footbridge. The truss spans 32.5 m[5] and is made from untreated pine.

Fig. 7. Sawmill Creek covered bridge, Albert County, Canada.

The Pyrmont Bridge at Darling Harbour in Sydney was opened in 1902 as a vehicle bridge. In 1981, traffic was diverted to an adjacent freeway and it has only been used as a pedestrian and cycle bridge since then. The bridge which is 390 metres long consisting of 12 spans built on ironbark Allan trusses and a centre steel swing bridge. The bridge was renovated in the 1980's and while some members had to be replaced, this was mainly associated with poor maintenance allowing the ingress of moisture and poor maintenance of paint.[6]

Fig. 8. Pyrmont Bridge, Sydney.

---

[5] Government of New Brunswick. Transport and Infrastructure. http://www2.gnb.ca/content/gnb/en/departments/ dti/bridges_ferries/content/covered_bridges/albert.html. Date accessed August 26, 2015.

[6] Thurman, E.G. Pyrmont Bridge – Construction & Restoration in Engineering Heritage Committee, Sydney Division, Institute of Engineers 1991. *Proposal to Landmark the Pyrmont Bridge, Darling harbour as a national Engineering landmark.* URL: https://www.engineersaustralia.org.au/portal/system/files/engineering-heritage-australia/nomination-title/Pyrmont_Bridge_Darling_Harbour_Nomination.pdf. 41.

The timber in these three bridges succeeded because they were protected from the elements, the first two by a roof, and the third by a deck. A timber bridge, detailed well to shed moisture instead of trapping it in joints, is a durable structure and can hold its own as a viable option alongside other materials. This book will show you how to detail to achieve that end.

The new materials of steel and concrete were rated for longer than timber but the USA experience was that they were not found to perform as expected, whereas new timber products and processes have seen the one relegated material upgraded. It was reported in 2002 that of the 600,000 bridges in the US of which only 7% were timber, "240,000 were classified as structurally deficient or functionally obsolete."[7] This dire state of affairs forced the US congress to introduce the timber bridge initiative. Certain styles of timber bridges in the USA can now be certified for 75 years against the design life of 50 years for steel and concrete. These rapid advances have been slow to filter through to the Australian scene. So, what can you achieve if you are prepared to do things well but without putting a roof on your bridge? For your main supports you should be able to aim for at least 75 years, and now even 100 years as the upper level if you do things very well. But to do this you have to leave old and discredited practices behind.

No-one says, "We know how much it costs to do a bridge badly with timber, and we know how much it costs to do it with steel or concrete, but how much does it cost to do it very well with timber?" Here is an example – in 2013 we quoted $150,000 for a 50 x 3.0 m long assembled bikeway bridge superstructure built on log girders to replace a similar 100 year old bridge washed away during the 2011 floods. This was about $1000 per m^2 With installation, it would not have gone above $1700 m^2. Make no mistake, this would have been a very good bridge. Concrete was used instead and the reported installed price was

Fig. 9 Timber highway bridge under construction in the USA rated for 75 year life.

$5,560 per m^2. Is there a balance in between? I believe so. A 100 year life laminated timber beam bridge would have come in at about $2,500 to $3,000 per m^2 installed.

So timber should not be dismissed. However, we must be prepared to use the medium well.

When it comes to long span footbridges, timber is not just one material among others to choose from. This is an area in which timber can excel over alternatives. The January 2011 floods in Queensland saw a big change in bridge enquiries. After many years of drought, we had forgotten that sometimes it rains very heavily indeed. When designing a bridge, every effort should be made to keep its feet dry. When the floods came, many bridges simply disappeared. Before the flood, it was unusual to have enquiries

---

[7] A contributing factor to this premature failure can be the practice of putting salt on the roads, a practice to which timber is relatively immune. A further contributing factor is the freeze–thaw action to which again timber is not vulnerable. Freedman, G. *Timber* …, 16, 40. Another contributing factor has been bad design, something which can happen with all materials, but is forgiven when the medium is steel or concrete rather than timber.

beyond a 24 m span but then we were being asked for 50 m and even a 90 m clear span. But what were your options when you wanted to span these distances when often the dead weight of a concrete or steel beam makes a simple span in these materials impractical? It is helpful to consider how alternate materials could be used to achieve these spans and compare them to timber.

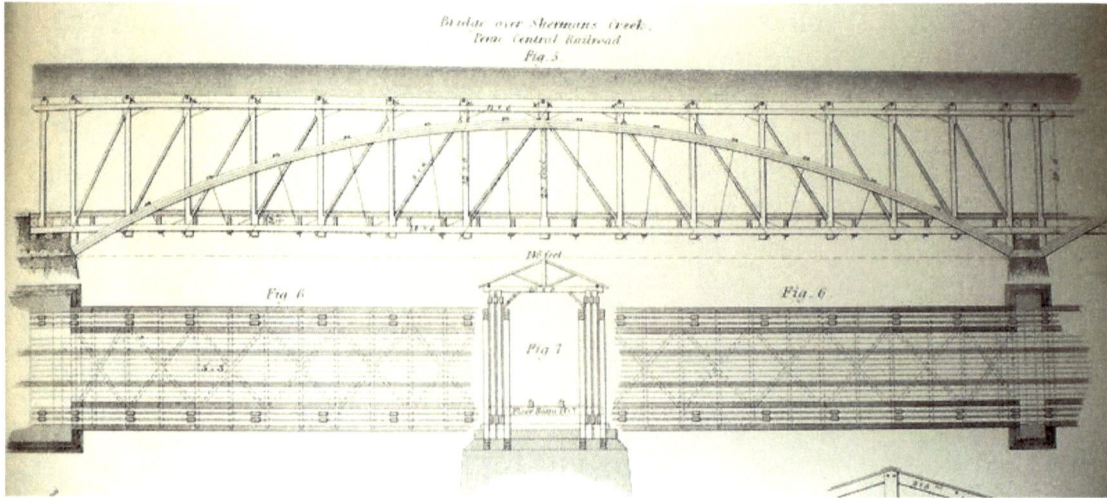

Fig. 10. Timber bridge over Sherman Creek (148 ft) Penn. Central Railway drawing C.1880.

Fig. 11. Clifton Bridge near Bristol UK.

Fig. 12. Szechenyi Bridge in Budapest.

Fig. 13. 320 m suspension bridge in Japan with timber decking supplied by the author.

In my grandfather's book on carpentry and joinery from 1880,[8] there is information on how to build a 45 metre span Burr arch truss railway bridge using timber trusses. Impressive as this is, it is a long way short of the 90 metre span we were asked for. Suspension bridges were a popular answer to these very long spans and many have proved very durable. These bridges require all the loads to be transferred back into the banks and so, ideally, require rock at each end to make the necessary connections. They can be very attractive bridges as the bridge by Brunel at Clifton (Figure Eleven) and the Szechenyi bridge in Budapest (Figure Twelve) show but there are many places they simply can't be built.

Timber has mixed success in these applications in Australia. For recreational paths where budget priced bridges are required, suspension bridges are frequently under designed and very appropriately sometimes called "swing bridges"[9]. Structures that are, quite literally, life threatening have been built and not always in timber. Fortunately, suspension bridges are not always like this as the 320 m bridge in Japan (Figure Thirteen) for which we supplied timber shows. But the cost to build a robust structure like this is very high.

Fig. 14 Cable stayed bridge by the author at Berrinba Wetlands, Logan.

A more adaptable and even more attractive arrangement to a suspension bridge is a cable stayed bridge. The two bridge types are frequently confused. Instead of the load being transferred to the bridge approaches, they are carried within the bridge itself. So long as you can get a good foundation for the pier/piers only a standard abutment is needed at the ends. They can be striking architecturally and would be the natural choice if you require an "iconic" bridge as opposed to the most cost effective option. There is considerable scope to build these in timber. The cable stayed bridge shown in Figure Fourteen is probably close to a million dollars at the time of writing.

---

[8] Newlands, James. *Carpenters and Joiners Assistant*. (London: Blackie and Son. 1880).
[9] The colloquial term is not to be confused with a true swing bridge as seen in the Pyrmont Bridge – Figure Eight.

Fig. 15. 52 m span aluminium bridge, Jindalee.

Fig. 16. 40 m span bridge Brisbane.

Fig. 17. Standard Warren Truss as was supplied by the author with a 22 m span, Ipswich.

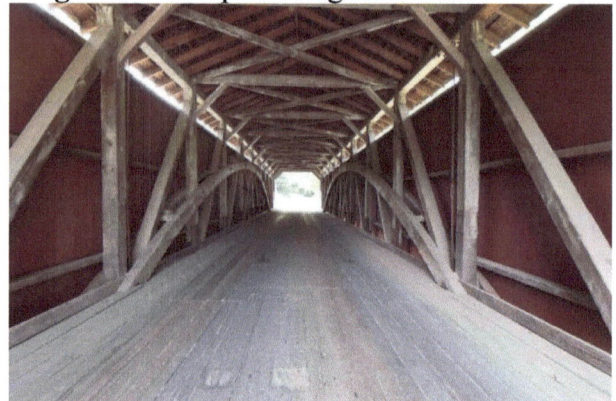

Fig. 18. Inside of 32 m span Baumgardener's Bridge, Pennsylvania.[10]

Trusses are an excellent method to span long distances as they avoid the massive dead weight of a simple beam. The range of truss types is vast. They all have different advantages, e.g. a Warren Truss is probably the most aesthetic but a Howe Truss is more efficient and will span further with the same member sizes. Trusses can even be architectural as well as functional. A well designed Warren Truss falls under that category as does the bridge by Bligh Tanner above (with shades of the Sherman Creek timber bridge illustrated in Figure Sixteen). Trusses are available in timber, steel, aluminium and fibre composite. The Bridge Code requires truss bridges to be U frame construction, (i.e. the rigidity of a transom to the vertical truss member is utilised to elastically laterally support the top chord) and it is all but impossible to achieve this in a light bolted construction. Failure to adequately achieve the required U frame action may be why many light trusses, whatever the material, shake when you walk on them.

Long span timber truss bridges have been used in covered bridges in the US and Canada and it is not unusual to get over 100 years service from them despite being built from untreated pine. Why, given Australia's harsh climate, we never adopted covered bridges, I cannot understand. (I suspect that it was because the timber was so durable and gave reasonable service despite often being used inappropriately that designers were not forced to explore what best practice is).

---

[10] This double Burr arch bridge was built in 1860 and restored in 1987 after flood damage.

The aluminium truss featured in Figure Fifteen is an excellent example of construction in that material but, if aluminium has a weakness, it is the high cost to do well with stiffness that complies with the Bridge Code. I have not been impressed with some kit aluminium bridges due to stiffness issues. Our preference would be for a fully welded structure with a splice, if absolutely necessary, for transport. This does away with bolted connections and gives a far more rigid structure. Remember, gangways are not footbridges and should not be purchased to serve as such.

Whereas a simple log girder bridge could perform without any trouble despite going through repeated inundations, suspension and cable stayed bridges must all be above the flood level. Trusses, likewise, should be above the flood level as their strength is vertical, not horizontal.

Fig. 19. 120 metre clear span timber footbridge.[11]

While we supplied some magnificent kit steel framed bridges as some of the figures have illustrated, I have to confess my love affair with timber. New generation timber products are adding a completely new dimension to what is now possible in a long span bridge. I first wrote about a request for a 50 m and even 90 metre clear span but what do you do when asked for 120 metres? This is where timber stands head and shoulders above its competitors.

---

[11] This bridge which was a joint effort between OSA and Timber Restoration Systems. It did not go ahead due to the client's nervousness over timber.

2. Timber for Footbridges

Pine or Hardwood?

Fig. 20. Soil up against the frame.

Fig. 21. Subsequent decay.

Fig. 22. Fire Damage.

Fig. 23. Nailplates working out.

The bridges in Figures Twenty to Twenty-three are made with pine. Pine can be prevented from decaying by using the correct treatment but the Queensland experience is that pine bridges are not lasting Constant wetting and drying causes the pine to self destruct in the harsher climates. That is very different to decay.

Pine bridges need far more care with their detailing than one built of the most durable hardwoods. The bridges in Figures Twenty and Twenty-one are made with timber treated to H3 (external above ground). The low cost and inadequate abutment has meant that soil comes onto the timber turning it into a H5 application (external in ground) and the life is immediately halved. As well, pine burns easily and nailplates are forced out more easily than in hardwood.

If you are prepared to cover the bridge as with the old bridges of North America, and combine that with preservatives and fire retardants[12], you will have a very good bridge that will outlast steel or concrete. If not, I would recommend durable, fire resistant hardwood. Laminated beams made from pine are a different case and will be considered in the chapter on laminated beams.

Specifying Hardwood

Fig. 24. Interior of Sawmill Creek Bridge.

In the *Background* section I mentioned that the first thing we had to do when becoming a footbridge manufacturer was to abandon the F14 specification. On the other hand, we have professional offices that say to me, "We will only specify according to Australian Standards." Why am I advocating timber use away from what is now the accepted norm? Over my career I saw the introduction of stress graded hardwood. Not all mills welcomed this, particularly the smaller producers who prided themselves on the high quality of the timber they produced and saw this as a lowering of standards. It had to be admitted that timber quality was variable from mill to mill. (Now we have stress graded timber, it is still variable from mill to mill.) I remember one article in our industry magazine saying that we did not have to be frightened of stress grading as now we could sell timber that was considered once unsaleable. Now, not only are we are seeing on the market timber quality that the better mills considered wrong, we are also seeing species used in applications that would never have been considered prudent before stress grading. And all of this is being driven by specifications like F14 and F17.

In Queensland, in my own structures, I expected a 20-25 year design life for our decking. The design life software predicts an 85 year life for our hardwood joists and bearers detailed the way we recommend[13]. This assumes doing nothing to the timber apart from an initial oiling. I am aware that these life spans are different from many designers experience or expectation. From our years of experience and formal research, we have a good understanding of which parts of the Standards we have to supply to are simply wrong or misleading. A fairly standard timber specification says something like F17 hardwood, treated to H5, Durability Class 2. It sounds good as three Australian Standards are alluded to. In reality, it says nothing meaningful! Consider timber specified as F14 or F17 to AS 2082. This is simply a specification of strength on the day of milling, nothing more. The properties you need are durability, stability, shrinkage and appearance, none of which are covered in timber that is simply

---

[12] Research the appropriate fire retardant with the chemical supplier as some retardants can promote decay.
[13] Refer to my book *Deck and Boardwalk Design Essentials* for details.

sold by an F rating.[14]   If purchasing on price, you are not assured of getting the species with the properties or physical appearance you want as they are usually more expensive.

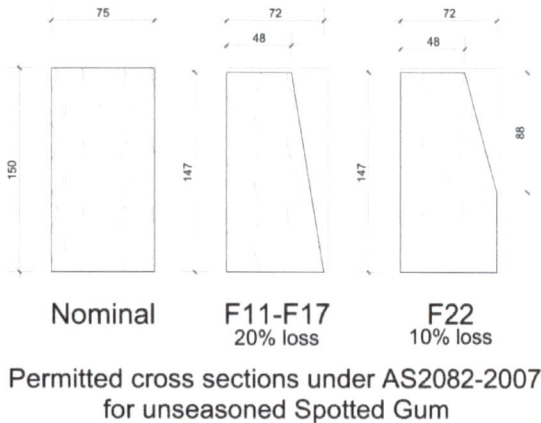

Fig. 25. Theoretical Cross Sections to AS2082.

Fig. 26. Treatable sapwood (highlighted red) in a pack of 200x100 mm.

It is also little understood that it is impossible to "preserve" sawn timber. It is only possible to treat sapwood, not heartwood, by commercial waterborne preservatives such as CCA, Tanalith E or ACQ. Consider the following. I can take a piece of blackbutt, a low Durability 2 In Ground timber, without any sap and paint on CCA with a paintbrush. Despite that being a total waste of time, I am then allowed to stamp that member as a H5 (in ground structural) piece of timber. Further, I can then dress that same piece of timber and remove all traces of the green colouring and I am still entitled to call that a H5 piece of timber! It clearly isn't preserved yet AS1604.1 (Specification for Preservative Treatment Part 1 – Sawn and round timber) is satisfied and would claim that it the equal to a piece of grey ironbark containing a little sapwood. Figure Twenty-five above shows what a piece of F11 to F17 spotted gum theoretically looks like allowing for permitted want and wane. There is 20% of its cross section missing. Sapwood on heavy joists and bearers is seldom more than 15%. This means that if the timber is not treated at all, it invariably will still meet the structural requirements! How long the member lasts will have nothing to do with its H level of treatment but its natural durability!

---

[14] Refer to my book *Grading Hardwood – Understanding AS 2084* where the omissions for products suitable for footbridge decking and structural members are elaborated upon.

Fig. 27. Garo Garo (so called Pacific tallowwood) sold as an In Ground Durability 3, timber, Above ground Durability 2 timber after 4 years in North Queensland (later downgraded to Durability 4).

The natural durability ratings (AS5604) are also a problem. This can be because of specifiers who have not kept up with the change to the standard – durability ratings are now classed as In Ground and Above Ground durability. If you specify the old way, say Durability Class 2, the supplier can say, "This is an above ground application. Therefore it is an Above Ground 2" and supply an old In Ground 3 timber (as illustrated above). These In Ground 3 timbers never were acceptable and remain unacceptable despite ticking the correct boxes. Further problems arise through the wide spread of durability within a group. Above Ground 1 will pick up Blackbutt. Yet, in Queensland, it is not considered suitable for a railway sleeper, crossarm or for timber bridges (other than a deck under a bitumen running surface). These are applications where timber species performance has been monitored. How can it now be suitable for a light bridge? The life expectancy figures in the Standard also bear little relation to reality when it comes to decking and the fine print in the Standard about their accuracy is not given due attention. The old designation of Royal Species for those few species that perform well above the rest has been lost or totally misappropriated to inferior timbers.

So, timber specifications have to go far beyond Australian Standards, and we find many designers have a great reluctance to do this. The designer has to be an expert in timber design and few are. That is why we developed the safer path of proprietary products such as Deckwood. But taking the trouble to go beyond the standards will be rewarding, both financially and in supplying a structure that ages gracefully. But how do you do this?

Species Selection

There are over 200 species of hardwood milled commercially in Australia. Their properties vary dramatically. Some are suitable only for making disposable pallets and dunnage while a very few are among the best hardwoods in the world. Some species have very high shrinkage (e.g. turpentine) but are very durable and stable when kiln dried. However, turpentine is only harvested in small quantities. Fortunately, some of the best timbers for bridge timbers are among the most commonly harvested, at least in Queensland, and are sufficiently common in New South Wales.

Species	% of sawlog from Qld State forests	% of sawlog from NSW State forests	Royal species	Durability above ground	pH class[15]
Spotted gum	68.81%	5.90%	Yes	1	2
Broad-leaved red ironbark	7.02%	2.01%	Yes	1	3
Narrow-leaved red ironbark	4.60%	Ironbarks not separated in NSW reports	Yes	1	3
Grey ironbark	4.45%		Yes	1	3
Tallowwood	0.92%	1.27%	Yes	1	3
Gympie messmate	1.23%	0	Yes	1	3
Forest red gum	2.66%	.01%	No	1	2
Grey box	1.57%	0.08%	Yes	1	3
White mahogany	1.42%	.047%	No	1	3
Grey gum	0.61%	0.30%	Yes	1	3
Red mahogany	0.43%	0.40%	No	1	3
Kwila/Merbau	Imported		N/A	1	2

Table 1. Availability, royal species, durability and pH class.

I have mentioned the term "royal species". This has been defined as "A collection of eucalypt timbers which command a premium in price because of their great durability and strength".[16] But what constitutes this collection? I have met people who claim to have a seen a definitive list but no one has been able to point me to a document where it can actually be found.[17] Until I can find such a list, the prevailing and probably correct view is that this was a marketing term adopted by the industry. An old (90 years plus) senior forester recalled it this way - to be a royal species the timber had to be:

---

[15] Nguyen, Minh N, Robert H. Leicester, and Chi-hsiang Wang. *Embedded Corrosion of Fasteners in Exposed Timber Structures* (Forest and Wood Products Association: Melbourne 2008) 19-20.

[16] Anonymous. *Dictionary of Timber Terms* (Timber Secretarial Group: Sydney U.D.) 12.

[17] The closest I have come to a list is found in the Road and Traffic Authority report *Timber truss road bridges - A strategic approach to conservation, July 2011* where it says on Page 16 "These bridges need 'royal' species (Grey Box, Ironbark, Tallowwood and Grey Gum) as used in the original designs. Lesser timbers such as Blackbutt or Spotted Gum are inferior, have less strength and deteriorate at a faster rate, thus requiring more frequent replacement" (New South Wales Government, July 2011). The report can be found at http://www.rms.nsw.gov.au/documents/projects/key-build-programs/maintenance/timber-truss-road-bridges/timber-truss-road-bridges-report-july11.pdf. Spotted gum would be a sought out species for bridge work in Queensland but this may well reflect the variability between fast and slow grown timber.

- Highly durable
- readily available
- extractable and
- have a ready market.

The significance of the last three points is that the timber was not a "boutique" or "craft" species that is not available in large enough quantities to be commercial. For structural timber, royal species included grey and red ironbark, spotted gum (above ground applications), tallowwood and yellow stringybark. The list varied from state to state and in Western Australia included jarrah and karri despite being of lower durability than the eastern Australian list.[18]

Unfortunately, on searching for this term on the internet, I found some mills in New South Wales advertising very inappropriate species as being "royal". So a very useful description has been devalued and effectively lost. You cannot go wrong with the old forester's list as far as durability is concerned. You can go wrong when you then insist on a species that has low availability.[19] You can go wrong also when you choose a species on colour and not on durability. My preference would be for spotted gum because of its ready availability and natural oils with the slower grown Queensland sourced material being preferrable.

Preservation

For hardwood, preservation should be considered the third line of defence after correctly specifying a durable species and giving close attention to detailing. With pine, preservation is the first line of defence. The sapwood of all species is rated as In Ground and Above Ground Durability Class 4. This means that the sapwood of ironbark is rated as the same durability as the sapwood of pine. Preservation of the sapwood is essential for all species, lyctus susceptible or not, when used externally. But note that I said preservation of sapwood, not the timber.

---

[18] Smith, Walter. *Pers. Com.* Jan 18, 2013.
[19] We quoted a large quantity of tallowwood architectural battens shortly before writing this book. This species makes up less than 1% of the Queensland forestry harvest but it is more common in NSW. We found one NSW mill that may have been able to supply at the future time required and another that could guarantee supply. There was 20% difference in price between definite and maybe. If costed on a possibility, it may have caused major problems at the time of supply.

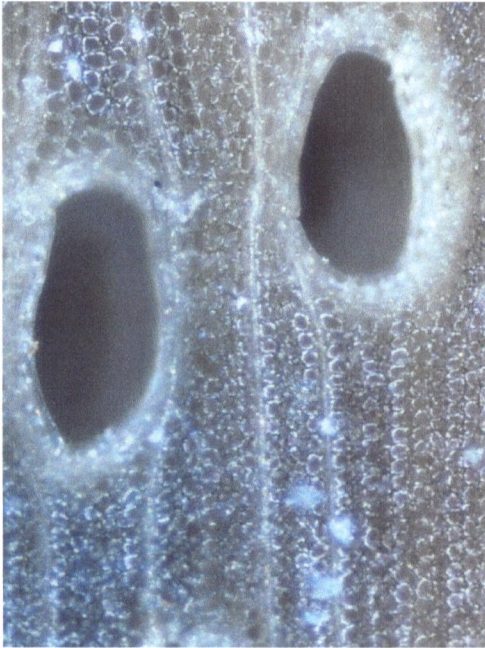

Fig. 28. Empty sapwood vessels.　　　**Fig. 29.** Closed heartwood vessels.

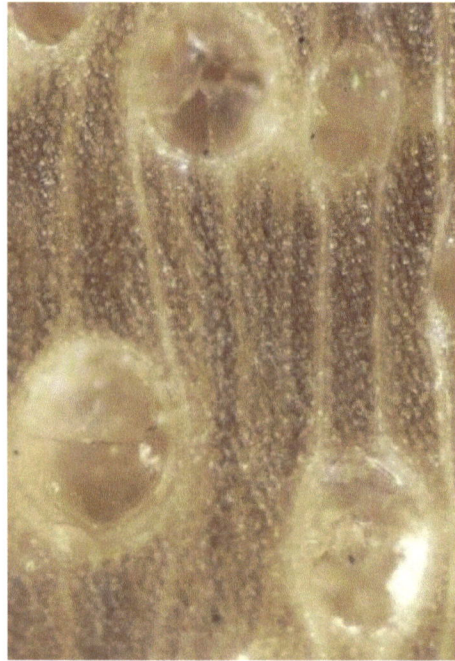

Figures Twenty-eight and Twenty-nine show the sapwood and heartwood (also called truewood) of tallowwood. It is evident that the vessels in the sapwood are porous allowing the treatment chemicals to flow through them. By contrast, the vessels in the heartwood are plugged. These occlusions are called tyloses. **Timber preservation only works on sapwood**. It has absolutely no effect on the heartwood whether pine or hardwood. The old adage states that "You cannot make a silk purse out of a sow's ear". And in like manner, you cannot raise the performance of the heartwood of non royal sawn timber such as blackbutt through preservation. You can only stabilise the sapwood. Preservation must be viewed, not as the primary means of achieving durability but as an enhancement of timber with already naturally high durability.

The application is H3, (external above ground) so it gives you a number of options for the type of preservation. These are:

- waterborne
  - CCA
  - ACQ
  - Tanalith E
- solventborne
  - LOSP

There are restrictions on the use of CCA imposed by the Australian Pesticides and Veterinary Medicines Authority (APVMA)[20] but bridges, including their commercial style decking, are not a restricted use so it is possible to receive CCA treated timber if care is not taken. As well, there is some concern in the industry about the effectiveness of LOSP used externally. You need to specify either:

---

[20] Any product claiming to be a preservative has to have its evidence verified by the APVMA.

VPI[21] treated to H3 with ACQ or Tanalith E, CCA and LOSP not permitted or
VPI treated to H4 with ACQ or Tanalith E, CCA not permitted.

If I was producing the bridge I would use the first specification. An engineer who does not have the control I have might specify the second option as a further guarantee not to receive LOSP treated timber. Can the timber be purchased without sapwood? Perhaps for smaller quantities but with great difficulty and much added expense. My personal philosophy is that ordering sap free is a **very irresponsible** use of a limited resource and you would be advised to go to an alternate material.

Timber Grade for Frame

After having determined the species to be used and the means of stablising the sapwood, you then have to consider the grade of timber you will use for the frame. Do not, at this stage, jump to an F grade.

When produced from the timbers of south east Queensland, the lower F grades are visually unacceptable.[22] Yet, we see some professional designers who just see a number with an F in front of it, asking for grades that are far lower than 38% of the strength of defect free timber[23]. Visually and structurally, they are appalling and durability can be all but non-existent. You would not specify steel or concrete this way and timber is no different.

Structural Grade:	% of clear wood strength
No. 1	75%
No. 2	60%
No. 3	48%
No. 4	38%

Table 2. Structural grades as a percentage of solid wood.

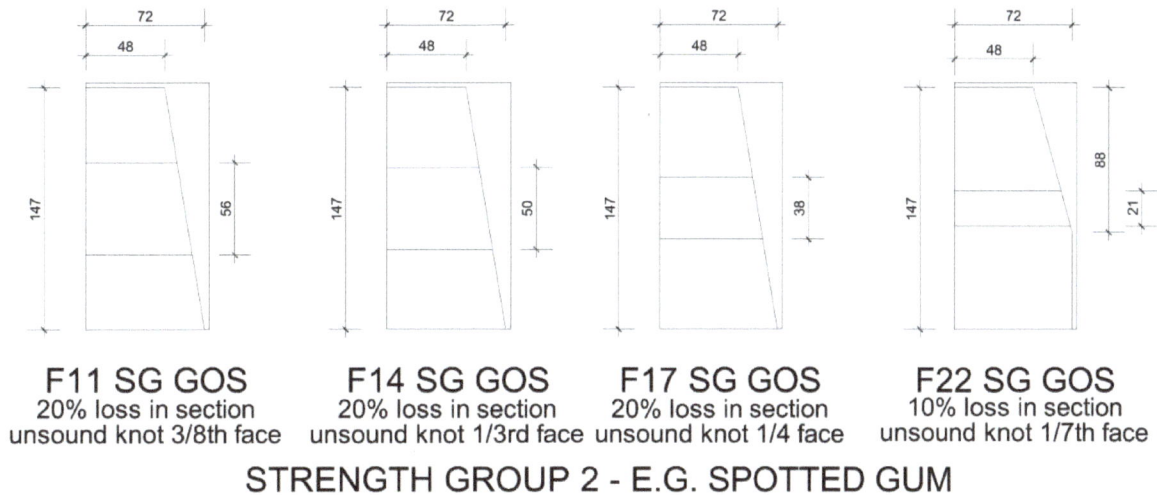

F11 SG GOS
20% loss in section
unsound knot 3/8th face

F14 SG GOS
20% loss in section
unsound knot 1/3rd face

F17 SG GOS
20% loss in section
unsound knot 1/4 face

F22 SG GOS
10% loss in section
unsound knot 1/7th face

STRENGTH GROUP 2 - E.G. SPOTTED GUM

Fig 30. Theoretical cross section of structural grades.

The lowest structural grade you should ever consider using in weather protected areas of the bridge is

---

[21] VPI is an abbreviation for vacuum pressure impregnation.
[22] Refer to Appendix 1 for an example of F grades not meeting visual expectation.
[23] Refer to my comments on F14 and F17 KD specification in my book *Grading Hardwood*.

Structural Grade 2 and that is not an attractive piece of timber if the defect is at its maximum. If you have a range of species, say ironbark (some are Strength Group 1) and spotted gum (Strength Group 2), you would work your calculations on the value given for lowest Strength Group which would be F17 for unseasoned timber. Your specification would be read something like:

200x75 spotted gum, ironbark or tallowwood in Structural Grade 2, for all species, sapwood Tanalith E or ACQ treated to H3. Independent confirmation of grade is required.

Fig. 31. How not to place your timber.

When constructing the bridge, the faces that have the most natural feature should not be placed on the outside of the bridge. Instead, protect them by placing them on the inside. Similarly, edge defects should be placed downwards.[24] For members that are more critical, such as those in trusses made from ex 50 mm members, the grade should be increased to Structural Grade 1.

Barrier timber

How do you specify timber for a toprail according to AS 2082 Timber - Hardwood - Visually stress-graded for structural purposes? Quite frankly, when our family was milling, we ignored the standard and just produced a product suitable for application. What is the correct way to specify it when you do not have access to your own sawmill? In Table Three, the defects permitted in two species (spotted gum and broad leaf red ironbark) in two of the best grades (F22 and F17 exposed) are compared.

Defect	F22 SG	F22 RI	F17 EXP SG	F17 EXP RI
Want and wane	10%	20%	No	No
Gum pockets	300 mm	300 mm	No	No
Loose gum veins	1/10th length	1/6th length	No	No
Tight gum veins	Unlimited	Unlimited	Unlimited	Unlimited
Sound knot	21 mm	38 mm	38 mm	50 mm
Termite galleries	Surface	Surface	No	No
Table 3. Comparison of different grades suitability for handrail.				

Neither F22 or F17 appearance grade is completely suitable for specifying handrail.[25] The exposed grade with unlimited tight gum veins and up to a 50 mm knot is too generous. A suitable specification

---

[24] The placement of natural feature away from the weather is important. I would pre-grade our hardwood and brand it but when I saw a "down" up and "inside" out, I realised that that was a waste of time and so discontinued the practice. Every piece should be assessed and used to produce the best performance.

[25] Refer to the Barriers chapter where there is a discussion of terminology. The term here is being used as understood in the trade.

for dressed timber handrail would be something like this:

Royal Species[26] (including spotted gum), Structural Grade 1, the order to the timber supplier is to state that the timber is required for handrail and to over-order by 10%. (This allows for 5% of the timber supplied being out of grade[27] and a further 5% is allowed for defects that are below the surface and will be exposed when the timber is dressed).

While this might seem extravagant, it really only means that a few of the longer lengths need to be ordered. The cost of setting up a planer a second time if you are a piece short is usually more than having spares. All timber by its very nature will have some natural feature so care needs to be taken how the rails are placed. Structural Grade 2 is adequate for the bottom face and defect on the edge should go to the outside.

Post Timber

Because the posts are aligned vertically, moisture is not retained so there is not the same risk of degrade as with the horizontal rail. Species choice is still critical. The same royal species as used in the rails should be used Structural Grade 2 (giving F17 in spotted gum and F22 in broadleaf red ironbark) may be adequate and an appearance grade would be better.[28] If you have no control over where the timber will be purchased, it is important that you specify appearance grade. Good building practice means that defect is aligned to the outside (refer to the case history, Boardwalk in Queensland in the chapter on barriers).

Decking

There are even more things to consider with decking and it is given a chapter of its own.

---

[26] Refer to my book *Grading Hardwood – Understanding AS 2082* where this term is explained. Some millers are now selling very inappropriate species as royal.

[27] AS 2082-2007 1.10.3

[28] The amount of defect allowed in Structural Grade 2 is very generous, e.g. 20% of the cross section can be missing. The mills we source from produce to a higher standard so I can quite safely purchase F17 spotted gum and it will be fit for purpose. Other mills push the standard to the limit.

3. Loads

The focus of this book is on what may be called a "park bridge", an area where non specialists regularly work and kit bridges are frequently used because of the shorter spans. All footbridges are not created equal. As much as we want there to be, there is not a one size fits all solution to the problem of footbridges. One bridge could be at a high level beside a main road from where a fall is almost certainly fatal. Another could be over a main road where the consequence of failure is much higher than normal. Another bridge could be kilometres down a remote walking track where there is no likelihood of disabled users or unsupervised children. Another could be a short low span in a park where its primary purpose is decorative. Yet another could be part of a large building complex where everything around it is built to the Building Code of Australia (BCA). Every bridge has to be assessed for its own particular needs.

Fig. 32. Wide variety of "park bridges" built by the author.

Bridge Vibration and Load Requirements

Fig. 33. Steel truss bridge needed bracing back to existing road bridge

Fig. 34 Timber truss that was braced to a road bridge but shattered when there was an accident on the bridge – replaced with steel a Warren truss by the author.

The images in Figures Thirty-three and Thirty-four are a cause for concern. These pedestrian bridges were purchased on the basis of lowest price and, while the structure may have appeared satisfactory at the time of purchase, you really have problems with a bridge when it has to get its stability by having a brace retrofitted to a nearby road bridge. We urge purchasers to exercise extreme caution when specifying bridges to ensure that they meet minimum performance and safety standards. I am still seeing requests for footbridge quotes at 3 kPa loading from potential purchasers to match the first quote they received.

On first reflection, the high design loads we will be describing can seem "over the top". We look at a footbridge and there is usually no one on them or perhaps two or three at most. But all that changes in an instant when that otherwise empty bridge has to accommodate a fun run and do it safely. A few years back one of my employees, a big Cook Islander, came to me very worried. He coached a local junior rugby league team. One evening, he took the boys on a road run which took them over a 30 m plus truss. He did not notice anything untoward as he ran across first so he could see his boys were running. Then the eleven boys started to run across

Fig. 35. High design loads are not theoretical!

the bridge and it shook so badly he shouted at the boys to get off as he thought it was going to collapse.

Imagine if it had been a fun run! Because you have no control over how the bridge will be used over its very long life you ensure it can meet any reasonable foreseeable expectancy.

Ideally, you should just be able call up AS5100 (Bridge Design Set) and all of this is taken care of for you but, that bridge was certified, as were the bridges in Figures Thirty-three and Thirty-four. We have found that it is necessary to draw attention to some specific performance requirements and loads in your specification and design. To assist you assess the suitability of a bridge, I have included in Appendix 1 a specification for a footbridge and Appendix 2 a specification for a bikeway. This document also doubles as a check list. The Appendix is particularly helpful as not every person involved with footbridge specification and design has access to the Code because a hardcopy costs over $1100.

Vibration

Get the vibration characteristics right and then basically everything else falls into place. The bridge must be designed so that the natural frequency is outside the problem vibration range which can be an annoyance in long span pedestrian bridges. You should specify at least 5 Hertz so it is far removed from a typical pedestrian walking speed. We find many specifiers are accepting of high vibration as they mistakenly think that it is normal, perhaps even acceptable. In addition, the stiffness of the decking influences the confidence a user has in such a structure. We confine decking movement to less than 1.7 mm under a 100kg concentrated (foot) load which was a criterion from the original AS 1684 (Timber Framing Code).

Applied Loads

There is NO allowance under AS 5100 for any reduction of the distributed load of 5 kPa until the element being designed is supporting an area greater than 85 m2. Then typically it only reduces to 4 kPa for girders of 40 m span bridges or longer. A lower load is only permitted for the footpath attached to a normal vehicular bridge and, in that situation, the footway area has to support a 4 tonne axle load anyhow, and that would tend to govern the design. A 3 kPa bridge is simply wrong.

When a tractor has to cross the pedestrian bridge it has to be designed for it, and that requires a wider bridge generally and a much heavier deck. If an alternative maintenance vehicle crossing can be found or a load limitation posted or bollards to restrict vehicle access, then there is no guidance from that Code so we have to resort to AS 1170.1 (Loading Code) where a 4.5 kN concentrated load is specified. This allows our bridges to carry a golf car or similar vehicle with no fuss.

Load Factor

Most structural codes in Australia now have Limit State approaches to design, so loads have to be multiplied by a Load Factor. AS 5100 requires a load Factor of 1.8 but will permit 1.5 for bridges NOT over public roads or railways.

Design Methods

Like the British Standard, AS 5100 specifies that a 'Through' bridge must have the compression element designed for restraint by the 'U Frame' method. Many designers are not aware that this significantly increases the 'effective length' of the top chord - typically double the nodal distance. (A 'Through' bridge is where the deck is at the bottom of the girder or truss. Almost all truss bridges are 'Through Bridges'.)

Barrier

Fig. 36. 20 mm solid steel balustrade transitioning to 16 mm aluminium – someone's engineering is wrong!

A normal bridge rail should be able to withstand 0.75 kN/m laterally and vertically (not crowd loading which increases to 3 kN/m). The stiffness specified is span (between posts) /800 which is difficult to achieve, especially with aluminium [low E value]. The barrier often becomes the most contentious part of a design. It needs to be higher and offset for cyclists and the Bridge Code requires it to be non-climbable. Some local authorities, recognising that typical fall heights of most pedestrian/cycle bridges are less than 4 m, adopt the view that a railing comparable to the building code would suffice. That component then is not included in the Bridge Code certification.

Walking Track Structures

If a bridge can be classified as a Walking Track Structure (AS 2156.2), then the design load could be reduced to 4 kPa but it would not comply with AS 5100. It would also have to support a concentrated load of 4.5 kN. For non-urban locations with infrequent walkers (refer to AS 2156.1) as in remote sections of National Parks, a Class 3 track is possible. Such a structure requires a 3 kPa loading and a 1.4 kN (140 kg) concentrated load provided it is not likely to be used as a viewing platform. The concentrated load is very similar to the 1.35 kN load from the British Code, being a walker with a full backpack. Outdoor Structures Australia makes two types of bridges for Class 3 tracks - a segmental bridge that can be carried by a quad bike and assembled on site and a robust tube bridge that is designed to be carried fully complete by helicopter. Both of these can carry a quad bike with ease.

Flood Loads

To reduce span and/or cost, many of our bridges have to be placed so low that a flood will inundate them. Most times, flood forces are significant but the barriers can be modified to reduce both the load on the bridge and to minimize the increase in flood level upstream. Obviously, catching debris is a problem for the damming effect and for the clean-up afterwards. Truss and suspension bridges are not appropriate in these situations.

Of course, it goes without saying that these criteria and more were all addressed in the footbridges I supplied which made them the most robust on the market. These comments are directed to public/commercial bridges. A domestic bridge would simply have to comply with AS 1170.1 (loads) and its barriers comply with the BCA.

4. Decking

Fig. 37. Untreated Sapwood.

Fig. 38. Cupping.

The requirements for decking go far beyond the requirements to timber produced to AS2082. Figure Thirty-seven shows untreated ironbark. The sapwood is identified as the lighter coloured timber on the edge of the boards. This timber would be classed as F27 if it is broadleaf red ironbark. But that sapwood will decay and leave a trip hazard. These boards should not have been used. In the same vein, Figure Thirty-eight shows ex 150x38 mm spotted gum clear of defect so it could have been graded as F22. This piece, with a 4 to 1 ratio of width to thickness will perform satisfactorily in a roof truss but, used as decking with a different moisture content on the top compared to the underside, it has cupped and is unsuitable as it will degrade quickly as moisture is retained. The ratio should not go beyond 3.5 to 1, e.g. 120x35 mm and 145x45 mm.

In my book, *Grading Hardwood – Understanding AS2082,* I argue the need for a specification just for decking. That book contains two case histories showing unsuitable timber being used. Some pieces have defects outside that permitted by AS2082 and others that are permitted but should not be used. I have included in Appendix A the specification I would use for our 145x45 mm Deckwood decking which you should use if you want to avoid issues. The two case histories I mentioned establish the need for independent confirmation of grade. Be very careful not to place in front of the decking specification F17 or F22. The Specification for an F rated structural timber and a suitable decking specification are two entirely different things.

Decking Alignment

Normally, decking is run crosswise and is the recommended practice. The reasons for doing so are because it:

- Utilises shorter and easier to obtain timber
- Has better slip resistance for pedestrians[29]
- Has less issues for bike riders
- Is easier to design.

---

[29] Testing done by the University of Southern Queensland for the author showed a significant difference between slip resistance walking across the grain of a natural sawn top surface compared to walking with the grain

While, in some designers minds, there can be a clear distinction between a bridge on a designated bikeway and one on a pedestrian bridge, this is not a distinction made by the general public. If there is a bridge, whatever it is officially called, people will ride a bike over it. At the very least, the deck should not pose an obstacle to bike use. Refer to Figure 41 for an example of unsuitable deck design for bikes.

Fig. 39. Poor design detail on footbridge with the deck running lengthways	Fig. 40. Using two transoms allows for a gap between the decking ends and screw end clearances.

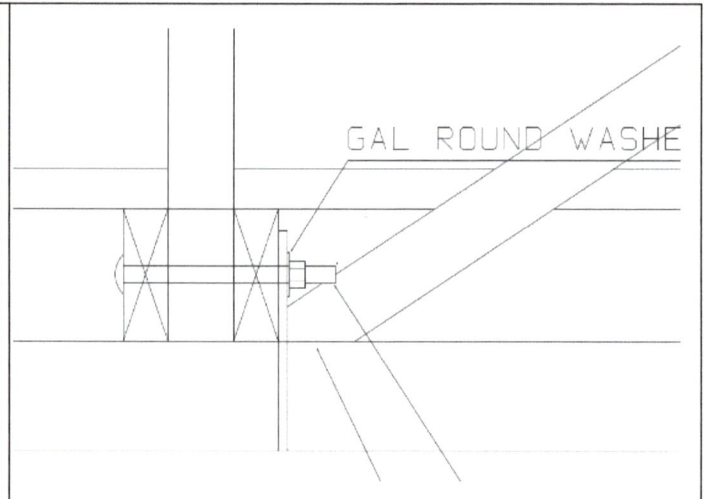

The deck can still be run lengthways but the decking must be seasoned to ensure that the gap is very small, no more than 5 mm in my opinion. Care also has to be taken to design the join in the decking. There must be a gap between the deck boards ends of about 5 mm to stop moisture entering the end grain and also end clearances on the screws must also be maintained. This requires joining over two transoms (Figure 40) not one as in Figure 39.

Gaps in Decking

Fig. 41. I had no trouble finding gaps of this size in a prominent deck in Canberra.

Fig. 42. One of my newsletter readers was injured by this 29 mm gap on the same deck.

In early 2005 I was sent a set of plans to quote the materials for a prominent deck in Canberra. As I looked at these plans I thought that this deck should not be built as originally drawn. I must say that the aesthetics were stunning but, from architectural intent to working drawings and specification, there were a number of issues. The main problem I saw was that the design utilised wide unseasoned decking laid with a gap. After seasoning the gaps had to well exceed that which is considered safe for the public. I wrote to the engineers and offered my assistance to make this high profile deck a success but. Unfortunately, the offer was ignored. In 2009, I was visiting Canberra and decided to see how the deck had performed and, of course, the mathematics are so basic that it had to fail the disability code and it had by a long way. I had no trouble finding gaps of 24 mm. I thought about whether I should say something to the asset owner, (that is what duty of care would demand) but then. against my better judgment. decided that no one would listen or care.

Unfortunately, one of our newsletter readers contacted me not long after to say that he, or more accurately his bike, had found an even wider gap on this same deck. Over the handlebars he went, stitches to the face and damage to his back. Tragically, no one would talk to me at the design stage when all that was needed were a few simple changes to make the deck meet basic safety standards. The asset owner was, as a consequence, forced to talk to a solicitor acting for my reader.[30]   Figure Forty-two establishes clearly that your decking should run crossways, not lengthways.

Maximum Gaps: Clauses from codes relating to gaps that you need to consider when designing decks are:

Part 13 of Austroads (which quotes from the Disability Code) section 2.1.4 which covers drainage and grated areas. These can only have a maximum opening of 13 mm wide and 150 mm long to prevent entrapment of wheel chairs and walking sticks; and,

Part 14 of Austroads section 8.5.1, grooves (and presumably even more so with gaps) are not to exceed 12 mm when parallel to travel. Refer table 8-1

So, if you are building a deck, you need to aim for a gap no bigger than 12 to 13 mm. How do you do this with unseasoned timber?

First: Set your target gap.

Second: Nominate your species. Spotted Gum and Ironbark are excellent decking timbers and only shrink 6%. If you just say something vague like F14 hardwood Durability Class 1 or 2, you can be dealing with up to 12% shrinkage! We do not recommend specifying Blackbutt which is very commonly done in NSW.

Third: Deduct your expected shrinkage from the target gap and that is your laying gap (if you have a minus figure then you have a problem!) You may have to adjust the decking width or be forced to use seasoned material.

Fourth: Ensure the builders straighten the boards as they lay them. A piece of 150x50 mm decking 4.0 m long can have spring of 18 mm. This plays havoc with your gaps.

---

[30] When I went to see the deck in December 2014 to photograph the repairs I was certain had taken place I was disappointed to see that the asset owner had not repaired the deck, just placed barriers around it to keep bikes out. It is still dangerous for wheelchairs, walking sticks and high heels. It is very easy to do well and very hard to have the will to rectify.

As a rule of thumb do not go above 145 mm wide unseasoned decking. If you lay without a gap your expected shrinkage with spotted gum is 9 mm. That leaves you 3 mm tolerance for spring or for areas where the boards are undersize. You will never make an ex 200 mm wide unseasoned decking, even with lower shrinkage species, fully comply with the code.

Fig. 43. Decking gaps must suit the footwear expected

Inappropriate Footwear: A 12 mm gap and 4 mm stiletto heels do not mix (yes, it does happen). In consultation with a Brisbane architect we supplied a deck for a university campus club where it was expected that high heels would be regularly worn. In that case, we used 70x35 mm Deckwood laid without a gap. The expected gap (shrinkage) was 4.2 mm. This has been a success.

While we might talk of 12 or 13 mm maximum gap to meet different codes, this size gap is far too big for situations where high heels can be expected. We might speak of inappropriate footwear but rather it is really a matter of inappropriate gaps.

Seasoned or unseasoned: If you want a narrow gap (3 mm say) with a wide board it simply has to be seasoned. In practice, the majority of decking does not need a narrow gap and so can be unseasoned. The difference between seasoned and unseasoned is more expense, more delays, usually poorly specified, not available from anything thicker than ex 50 mm and, most importantly, lots and lots and lots of greenhouse gases. There should always be heart-searching before specifying KD on anything over ex 25 mm. When specifying wider boards remember the width to thickness requirements – 200x50 cups.

Fastening Decking

Fig. 44. Screw placement on a 50 mm joist.

It is always far better for the timber to be fastened from underneath though I readily acknowledge this is not always practical when it comes to replacement. Shrinkage is never an issue regardless of thickness, which it definitely is on sizes over 45 mm, when face fixed. Further, there is no chance of moisture entering into the joist down the screw hole and causing decay. Good as this idea is, it is rare to see this done.

To stop the joist splitting when face fixing (and pine joists split just like hardwood), the screws have to be in a staggered alignment and you need to maintain at least 4 diameters from the edge. This means that the joist width starts at 75 mm. This is explained in more detail in my books, *The Seven Deadly Sins of External Timber Design* and *Deck and Boardwalk Design Essentials*. For better aesthetics, the screws should be 304 grade stainless, not 316. Tea staining is desirable to dull the shiny surface of the screws.

Controlling Trip Hazards

A high grade of 145x45 spotted gum decking will span up to 900 mm on a normal pedestrian footbridge so, with narrow bridges, say up to 1500 mm it is not uncommon for the decking to be at maximum span and overhang with the decking fastened at only two points. This is a practice that should not be followed. Timber can bow and, if graded for straightness to AS2082, with one board bowing up and the next bowing downwards a trip hazard theoretically develops at 800 mm. And that is only if the timber is to grade. The deck in Figure Forty-five spans 900 mm and the trip hazard measures 11 mm and has caused a trip. A centre

Fig. 45. Trip Hazzard in decking.

distributer ex 75x75 should be installed up the centre to tie it all together irrespective of whether it is within the limits of the span..

5. Hardware

Bolts

Soon after I had started specialising in bridges and boardwalks, I sent an employee to replace a piece of kerb on a boardwalk I had built just three months earlier. He came back with one of the bolts (Figure Forty-six) and expressed great concern to me. The bolt had corroded so badly that the galvanising had even broken away the tar epoxy paint we had used for additional protection. I had some bolts from the same

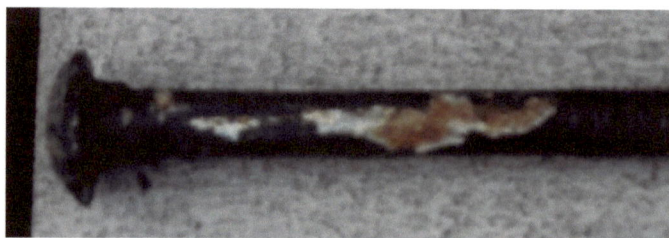

Fig. 46. New but rusting bolt.

batch and took them to Industrial Galvanisers (not the supplier) to see if they could tell me what was happening. Because the bolts were so bright the people at Industrial Galvanisers at first thought the bolts were electroplated and put a bolt through their laboratory to confirm. To everyone's surprise, they reported that not only were they hot dipped galvanised, they were well galvanised according to the standard. Having seen the old bolt, they were at a loss to explain why the galvanising obviously was not working.

Fig. 47. 51 year old galvanised bolt from Millmerran, Queensland.

Fig. 48 One year old galvanised bolt from Gatton Queensland.

When making choices about the bolt type, designers need to be very aware of the declining quality of galvanised bolts. The two bolts in Figures Forty-seven and Forty-eight are from similar timbers in a similar climate but the performance could not be more different. The old bolt still has its galvanising. Aggravating the declining quality can be the natural acidity of the some timbers – refer to the Ph class in Table One. Timbers in the Class 3 range can cause corrosion.

There is a full discussion of corrosion in fasteners in treated timber in my book, *Timber Preservation Guide* so here I give only the summary.

• Bolts, unlike screws, are supplied to a material specification, not a performance specification
• Advice on where to use galvanised bolts differs greatly among the various sources
• Real life testing in New Zealand has shown accelerated weathering tests do not reflect the results that will be achieved
• Real life testing recommends that if you are aiming at a 50 year design life you should use 304 or 316 stainless fasteners and
• Real life testing in New Zealand reflects the recommendation of Arch chemicals that external bolts within 8 km of the coast need to be stainless.

My recommendation to a specifier is to always use stainless bolts (or threaded rod where appropriate) but this is a case of do what I say and not do what I did. The commercial reality is that you could sell very few kit products with stainless bolts so, reluctantly, I generally used galvanised. When the

,application was right on the coast we would draw the line and invariably be beaten on price by someone supplying galvanised. As a specifier you have control over this. This is not to say there are not imported bolts that are as good as the old bolts. Your difficulty is in identifying them and then ensuring there is no substitution.

Brackets

Fig. 49. Australian bracket and imported bolts in a coastal location.

Australian made hot dipped galvanised brackets perform very differently to many of the imported bolts. Figure Forty-nine shows two bolts where the galvanising has completely gone and the heads are rusting but the bracket under it only has some white rust. The difficulty with galvanised brackets can frequently be the logistics. The fabricator has to take a standard size piece, cut it, punch holes, send to the galvanisers and possibly wait for hours to be unloaded, wait for the product to be galvanised and then possibly wait for hours again to be loaded. With stainless, you can design exactly what you want and have it all laser cut, holes and all to an accuracy of 0.5mm. All that is needed often is for it to be folded. The economics can be very good. For a more complete discussion consult my book, *Architectural Timber Battens*. The economics of using stainless can be surprisingly reasonable.[31]

Nailplates and Brackets

Fig. 50. Nailplates need to be closely screwed to prevent them working out.

Seeing the market gravitate to the lower price and longer span nailplated bridges, I decided I needed to have a nailplated bridge as well. The first obstacle was that our consultant refused to design one saying they were not certifiable. The second was that Pryda, whose products we used, refused to certify their products in that application. Their letter is included as Appendix B.

When timber joints are weather exposed, the connections need to be different to say, a roof truss, where the joints are not stressed by wetting and drying of the timber. The load carrying ability drops to a half when the plate has worked out just 2-3 mm. When nailplates are used they need supplementary fastenings such as closely screwing with stainless screws. This almost negates the purpose of using a nail plate in the first place.[32]

---

[31] As an example, I supplied a boardwalk with stainless steel wires that had a stainless spreader mid span so we could keep the wires at larger spacing. The quote to supply and install was initially very high and, when I queried it, the spreader with custom spaced holes were priced at $120 each – allegedly at cost price from their supplier. The company that provided our stainless brackets quoted us $17 in 2B grade 316 stainless and $34 polished.

[32] Another nail plate manufacturer advised me that, in conjunction with close screwing as advised by Pryda, another piece of timber over the top, also screwed, may well be needed. Smith. Matthew. *Pers. Com.* August 8, 2015.

The problem of nailplates being forced out is far greater with pine than hardwood but hardwood is not trouble free. I had made the same mistake with hardwood handrails on the log footbridges I made (refer Figure Fifty-one). I had to revert to just having the join on the post but I lost the end clearance I would normally use. Brackets on the outside would be preferable.

Fig. 51. Nailplates have also failed on hardwood.

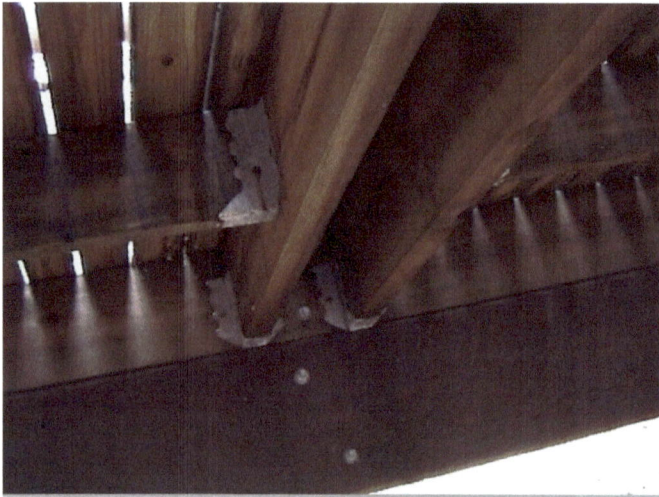

Fig. 52. Galvanised grips used in a bridge beside the water in Cairns.

Fig. 53. Corroded galvanised triple grip.

The use of any galvanised pressed steel connector in any external application is not an acceptable practice. The coating thickness is only 275 grams per m² (total of both sides). One major manufacturer, Pryda, requires stainless to be used for every external application irrespective of the distance from the coast. This advice is seldom heeded. Figure Fifty-two shows the underside of a footbridge installed in a marine application in Cairns in far north Queensland where the deck is supported with joist hangers used contrary to sound practice and manufacturer's recommendations. It has been observed that the more sheltered brackets can corrode more than the exposed ones and this is because contaminants are not washed off regularly.[33]

Stainless steel alternatives are available for many of the products and, while they are undoubtedly quality products sometimes, at least in the case of triple grips, are not always appropriate for bridge use. This is discussed and illustrated in my book, *Deck and Boardwalk Design Essentials*.

---

[33] Pryda. *Technical Update Corrosion Resistance of Pryda Products* Feb. 2012, 1.

Specialised Hardware

Unseasoned hardwood and pine shrink and, if we are talking large sizes, (above 50 mm thick with hardwood) we have to be talking unseasoned. Our dense Australian hardwood takes about one year per 25 mm thickness to stabilise. Without addressing shrinkage at the design stage you can find yourself retightening after six months and then yearly for a number of years afterwards. So it simply does not happen. The power authorities found a solution to this a long time ago in the form of the volute washer. We have been using them on our handrails for a long time. Overall, this is a very useful piece of hardware but it has been slow to enter the bridge field. In the chapter on handrail I give information on how to design and build with these washers.

Fig. 54. Crossarm hardware.

Another useful piece of powerpole hardware which can be incorporated when building a bridge with natural rounds is the gains block, also called crossarm mounting blocks, seen in figures Fifty-four and Fifty-five. They make an easy transition from round to square and are available in aluminium for sizes of 100 to 150 mm. Polymer versions are available for 75 mm.[34]

The use of a gains block is preferable to checking into the side of the girder which weakens the girder and traps moisture.

Fig. 55. Gains block

---

[34] Gains blocks are readily available from suppliers to the power industry. At the time of writing, one such company is G.V. Kinsman Pty. Ltd. (GVK).

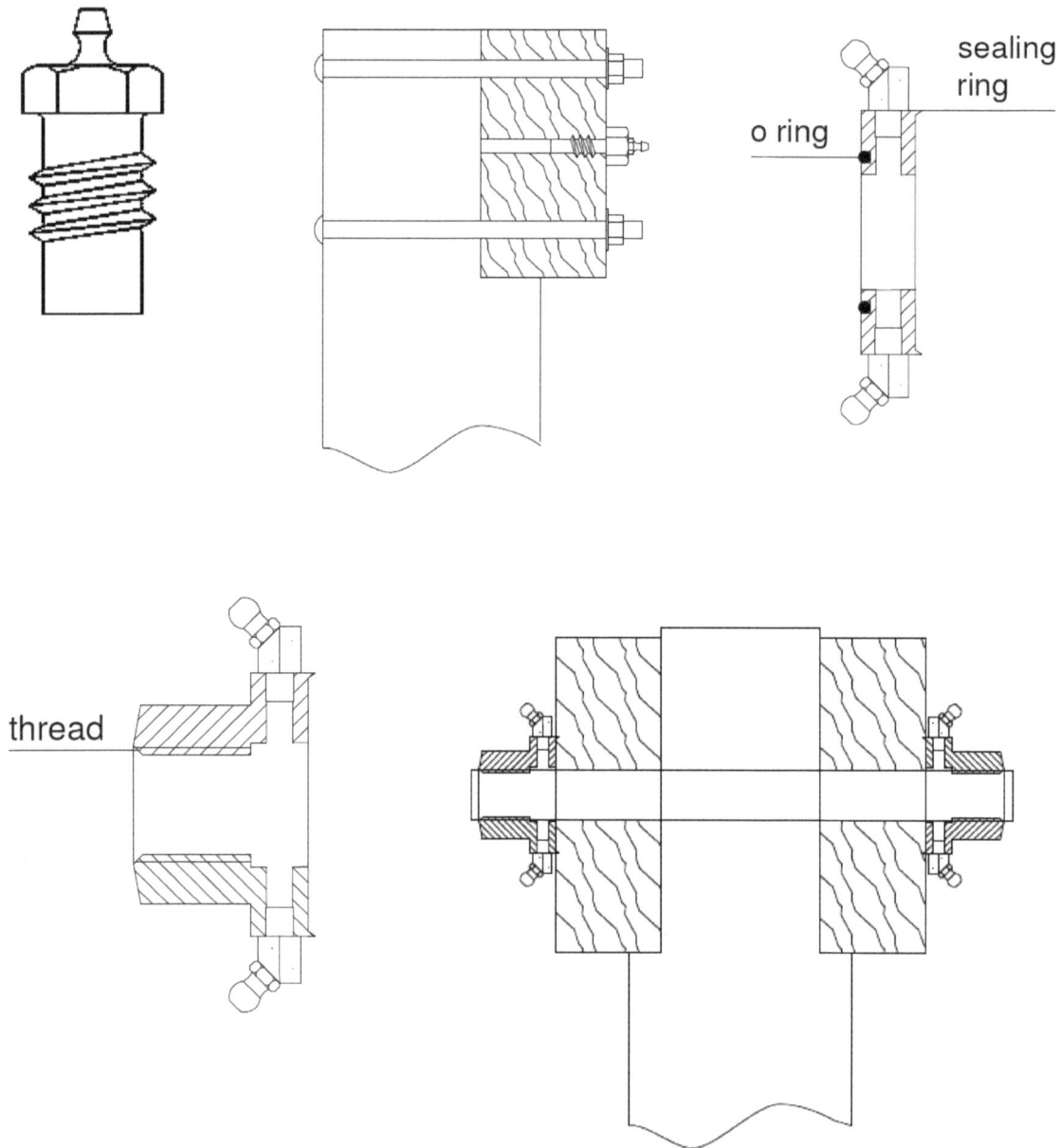

Fig. 56. Hardware designed by the author for introducing preservative emulsions into joints.

On hearing, in 1992, about problems with maintaining the joints in the historical trusses in NSW I designed a series of hardware items shown in Figure Fifty-six. The preservative grease like products, such as CN emulsion, could simply be pumped back into the joint during regular inspections. The wood nipple (top left hand item in Figure Fifty-six) was available for a time from one of the preservative manufacturers. All these products can easily be replicated on a CNC lathe.

6. Sawn Timber Joists

Fig. 57. Covered bridge built using sawn hardwood joists.

The subject of sawn joists begs the question when is a boardwalk a bridge and vice versa? Some applications are clearly bridges as Figure Fifty-seven. (This is the only covered timber bridge that I know of in the country.)[35] When the Walking Tracks standard was being developed, it was proposed that any span over 2.4 m would be classed as a bridge. The present wording is typically 1.5 m to 4.0 m though I have seen boardwalks built with 6 m spans. For most applications that involve simply supported sawn joists, the reader should refer to my *Boardwalk Design Guide* which has span charts for 5 kPA, 4.5 kN loadings up to 4.8 m span. That book, in conjunction with my *Deck and Boardwalk Design Essentials,* gives very detailed instructions on how to design boardwalk style structures. A further publication, *Boardwalk Construction Guide,* gives information about best construction practices. These publications mean that we can deal with the subject of sawn joists very briefly.

---

[35] I would appreciate feedback if you know of any others.

Fig. 58. Joist supported by a Barrup truss.

Large spans in hardwood require large heavy joists but not every bridge can be delivered assembled and then craned into position. Sometimes, timber simply has to be manhandled[36] down paths that are only accessible by foot traffic. The beam needs to be as light as possible. This can be done by incorporating a Barrup truss into the design. In our own designs it reduces a 250x100 mm member down to 150x100 mm. The difference in weight for a 6.6 m length is 200 kg compared with 120 kg.

A more complex but very effective alternative to the Barrup truss is to bond Kevlar or other reinforcing products to the bottom of the joist.

The issue of whether to use a dampcourse is not totally clear. In our early guides we recommended Malthoid for all applications.[37] This product glued to the joist and did effectively protect the joist, at least that is the feedback from builders doing maintenance on older structures in south east Queensland. Feedback from councils in the far north and from vehicle bridge maintenance specialists is that this same product can enhance decay. I suspect that part of that problem is that Malthoid has changed (I believe it is now imported) and no longer adheres to the top of the joist as in the past. The movement in vehicle bridges works against any bonding to the bearer. Products for use as dampcourse outside of the tropics that have promise are Norton Flashtac and Consolidated Alloys Byute Flash. These are both aluminium foils with a thick adhesive that bonds to the joist and seals the screw. In the tropics, there seems to be little doubt other than to let the joist breathe.

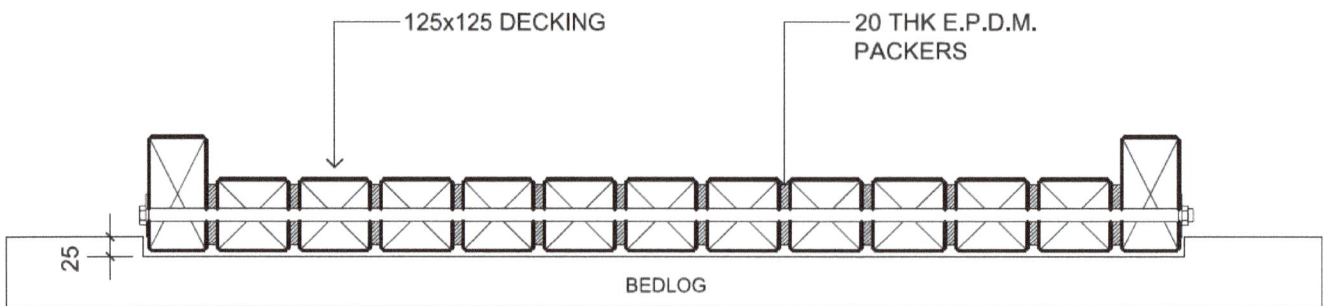

Fig. 59. Bridge built only of sawn "joists".

---

[36] From the Latin *manus* meaning hand, I am too old and too politically incorrect for person-handed.
[37] Malthoid is a 2-ply felt material impregnated with bitumen which is also covered in a fine sand to prevent sticking when rolled.

Occasionally, a bridge needs to be situated in a location where the creek is too "wild" during a flood to even contemplate the high cost of a structure sufficiently robust to withstand the flood forces, let alone the impact of a log. In these cases, it is a reasonable approach to build the bridge with as low a profile as possible and to attach a strong chain to it at one point. If the bridge is dislodged from its foundations it simply has to be levered back into place and re-attached. Figure Fifty-nine shows how such a bridge might look.

7. Log Footbridges

With scarce resources, Great Britain being six months away by sailing ship and infrastructure for a new nation having to be built on a very small budget, the very durable locally available hardwoods were the natural material for bridges. These timber bridges are now being overloaded tenfold from the horse and buggies they were originally designed for, despite being poorly maintained and poorly designed. In Queensland, timber highway bridges are still being reconstructed against plans drawn in 1936, despite the understanding of timber design having advanced dramatically since that time. Many of the remaining bridges are still giving very satisfactory service. No other material but timber could do this. And all this can be achieved by workers with moderate skills and basic tools.

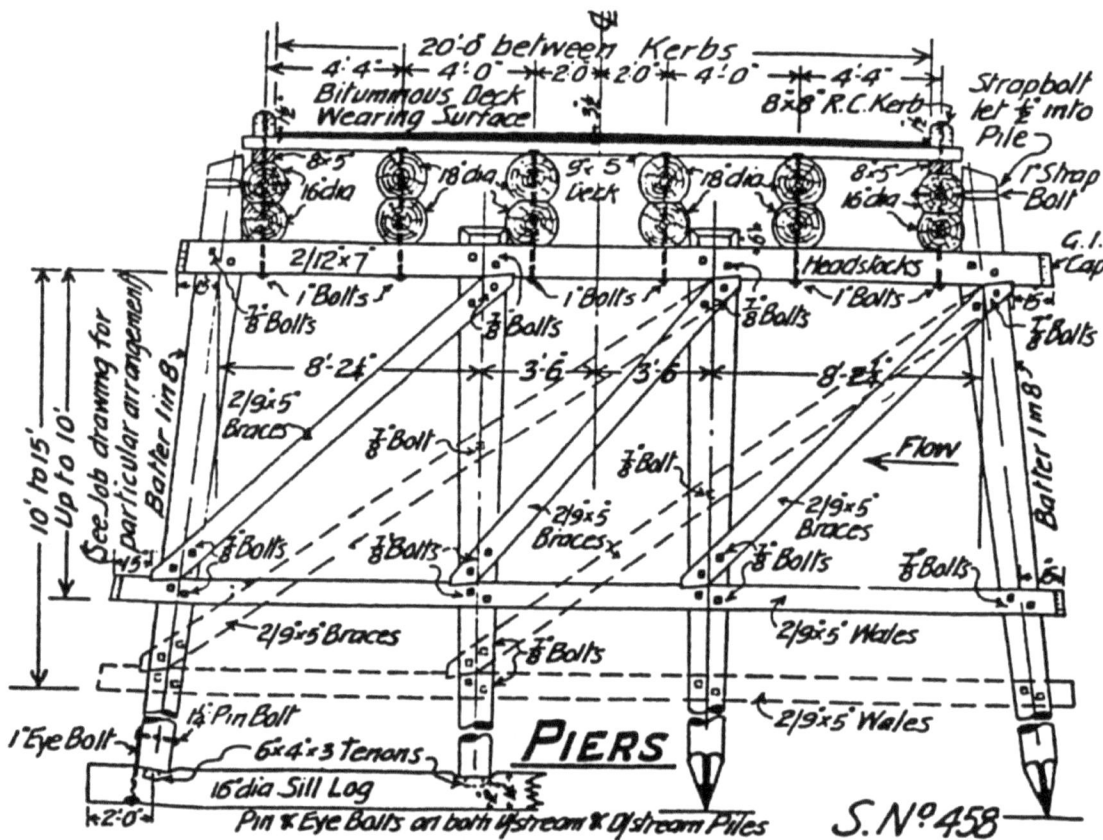

Fig. 60. A standard Queensland Main Roads bridge detail.

While there were a number of effective timber truss road bridges built from sawn timber, bridges were normally built from simple girders spanning 9 metres and spaced at approx 1.2 m apart.[38] A typical arrangement is shown in Figure Sixty. To allow for inaccuracies in construction, the girders join on corbels. Heavy headstocks connect driven timber piles. The life expectancies in Australia for these bridges are, decks - 10 to 15 years, girders – 20 to 30 years, pile bents 35 to 45 years. Despite the good service given, in Australia, authorities are more interested in managing the demise of timber bridges

---

[38] A typical A class road, 6.0 m between kerbs constructed of spotted gum would use 400 mm girders on the outside and four girders of 450 mm in the centre. The decking would be 225 mm wide, 125 mm thick and the headstocks would be a double 300x175 mm, Queensland Main Roads Department Drawing No 458.

with little thought given to extending their life. If best practice is adopted at construction or retrofitted during refurbishment, a life of 75 years can be achieved! [39]

What has been learned about road bridges is immediately transferable to footbridges. The girders are lighter of course but not massively. A nine metre long, 450 mm girder used in a road bridge would be replaced in one of our footbridges with an F27 (spotted gum) girder ranging from 375 to 400 mm measured at one third from the small end. The image of the concrete truck crossing a footbridge (Figure Sixty-one) is not so much a matter of the girders being oversized, but reflects the complexity of designing for crowd loading on footbridges. The reports of soldiers having to break march when they come to bridges are based on actual bridge collapses.

Fig. 61. Concrete truck using one of the author's log girder footbridge.

Fig. 62. Horizontal fixing of bridge girders and fastening decking from underneath.

Fig. 63. The inner three girders which have no decking bolts through them are in excellent condition but the outer bearers with vertical bolts have decayed.

Observation has shown that 10 changes to traditional bridge construction will assist in bringing about a dramatic increase in life expectancy of a footbridge built on girders. These are:

1. Change all vertical through bolts to horizontal, refer Figure Sixty-two. Any vertical fasteners should be from underneath and not penetrate the top surface
2. Do not use dampcourses. Let the timber breathe[40]

---

[39] Tingley, Dan. *Extending the Life of Hardwood Timber Bridges in Australia* a paper given at the 2014 conference of the Institute of Public Works Engineering Australia, Queensland for Far North Queensland.
[40] The use of dampcourses is discussed in Sawn Timber Joists.

3.   Incorporate positive drainage ensuring that moisture is shed away from any structural elements
4.   Provide for moisture content induced dimension change
5.   Do not band the top of piles
6.   Stop the use of drift pinning (anti split bolts)
7.   Provide proper clearance between timber elements
8.   Stop the use of heavy solid headstocks bearing on the top of the piles
9.   Stop the use of heavy notching
10.   Use proper size pile bents and place loads within D of pile to prevent horizontal shear cracking to undersized headstocks.[41]

Australian experience has shown it is possible also to build truss bridges spanning 90 feet (27.5 metres) predominantly using natural round timber. The truss illustrated in Figure Sixty-four was only taken out of service after 40 years when the road was upgraded. The 10 points above need to be adopted with the addition of not adding a metal cap to the top of the truss. This was done on a number of historical trusses in an attempt to extend their life but actually increased decay.

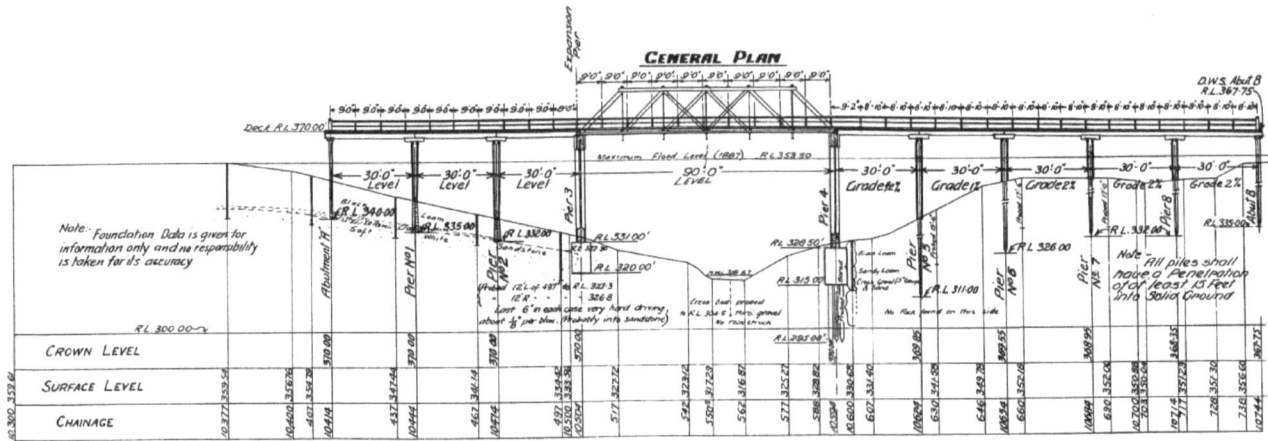

Fig. 64. Timber truss (27.5 m) built mainly from natural rounds.

Only the most durable species of high quality and straightness should be used as girders. The sapwood on the girders should be preserved. Frequently, the sapwood is removed by sawing the girder into an octagonal. While these octagonal are much easier to work on site, the girder is greatly reduced in strength. Paint is frequently applied in an attempt to extend the life of weather exposed structures such as bridges. Studies in Queensland have found that painted joints can retain moisture and decay actually may be up to three times as severe.[42] On bridges, it has been found that paint that has more than 29% solids traps moisture and can promote rather than prevent decay.[43]

---

[41] These 10 points and information on life expectancy are taught by Dr. Dan Tingley at the Advanced Timber Bridge Maintenance, Restoration and Inspection Practices Certification Course presented by Wood Research and Development.
[42] Francis, Lesley P and Jack Norton. Above-Ground Durability Estimation in Australia, Results after 16 Years Exposure, Document IRG/WP 05-20314. Paper given at the 36th Annual Conference of the International Research Group on Wood Protection, Bangalore. April 2005, 10ff.
[43] Tingley. *Extending...*, 42.

Fig. 65. 2x10m spans joined on a corbel built by the author.

Fig. 66. Single 10 metre span built by the author.

Because of their economy, I find logs very hard to go past for spans from 6 up to 8 metres. They are relatively inexpensive, usually less than steel and much less than laminated beams. Longer lengths can become considerably more expensive. They have the advantage of being strong in every direction.

Fig. 67. 15 m span laminated log footbridge built by the author.

Fig. 68. Keying girders together.

For spans up to 15 metres we have laminated two powerpoles with a light facing cut and then keyed them so they work as one unit. This design worked extremely well in its final form. We initially just bolted them together with shear plates at the interfaces and had seasoned hardwood keys set in epoxy resin inserted along the length. This did allow some sagging so the deck was built with a slight camber. The hardwood keys were changed to a 100x16 gal shear plate as the key but we had to make a machine that would form an accurate 110x15 vertical hole in the two girders. The laminated girder weighs at least 4 tonne beyond most yard forklifts so needs a larger crane to place the bridge girders. While this option should not be rejected out of hand by designers, there are many factors working against this option which need to be worked through. These are:

• The need for special equipment to make the groove
• If the bridge is fully pre-built it weighs about 10 tonne which can make lifting from the end a challenge on some sites
• The overall height of 1.0 metre is a disadvantage if the bridge goes under water
• Girders have to be individually selected for straightness.

A single 20 metre girder can be used (they are available in Australia as power poles) but these will deflect considerably under their own weight and need a Barrup or Finke truss to succeed. In the *Background* section of this book I recounted the story of a disastrous 20 m bridge we built. One of its problems was the truss did not work off the ends of the girders. With appropriate design, log girders can be used successfully in very long span bridges.

Girder selection and preparation.

Powerpoles are not girders! The harvesting practice in Queensland state forests is usually to cut the bridge girders first and then these are sold to the girder supplier at a very high price, then the powerpoles at a lesser price and the mill logs at a still lesser price. Quite often a powerpole is not sufficiently straight to be a bridge girder which is why they were sold as a pole and not as a girder in the first place. If you are not dealing with a reputable girder supplier who knows what must be supplied, it is important that you physically inspect each pole before delivery.[44]

Fig. 69. This powerpole was "crippled" by the facing cut and needed a retrofitted Barrup truss.

When you do your design, remember that girders are irregular and tapered. We design the bridges to accommodate up to 100mm difference between head and toe over all the girders in the structure. The logs are not an even taper but flare at the ground level and some logs flare more than others. At times, it is necessary to cut some of this flare from the butts to ensure they meet this difference. As mentioned, it has become very common to supply girders cut to an octagonal but this should be avoided as too much of the strength of the girder is removed. Apart from removing volume you have interrupted the grain of the timber. A natural round in spotted gum is F27 while a sawn structural member is usually classed as F17.

Case Histories

The two following case histories show that early engineers thinking about log girders went far beyond just a simply supported beam stopping at nine metres. There was innovative thinking back to the 1870's which pushed the boundaries of timber beams. These bridges were successful and had a long life. These styles of bridges appear to only have been built in Queensland.

---

[44] A service club in a city near to my home decided to give the city a footbridge (Figure 69). My girder price was far more than they were quoted for power poles. A couple of weeks after it was installed, the council approached me to design a Barrup truss for one girder as it was sagging badly. The facing cut which was slight at both ends virtually cut the girder to two thirds of its thickness at the centre.

Maclean Bridge over Logan River, with an overall length of 122 metres served as a road bridge for 60 years before being replaced in 1939 in concrete. The deck was 20 metres above the creek bed. It is sometimes thought that cable stayed bridges in Australia are a development post World War Two, but this bridge dates to 1880! It is reported that, "The drawings show that the old Maclean Bridge was a conscious design, with careful detailing of the tension rods and of the tall timber towers."[45] The centre span is 30 metres and the spans each side are 18.3 metres.[46] Despite being a success, no other bridge of this type is known to have been built in Australia.

Fig. 70. Cable stayed girder bridge over Logan River at Maclean

Fig. 71. Finke truss bridge near Yamba, Queensland.

Another remarkable bridge built on girders is the Finke truss built over Alligator Creek near Yamba, north of Rockhampton. It has been described as a "timber girder bridge with a complicated system of understrutting and diagonal metal ties. Timber posts were placed beneath the deck at one sixth points. From the base of the central post diagonal ties ran to each end of the main girder, and also to the top of the adjacent post on the midspan side. The span length was in the order of 36 m. Unfortunately it has not been dated, but for many years it was notorious as a danger spot on the northern highway".[47] It is not surprising that this bridge was intimidating for vehicles as it was designed for horses and carriages yet it served for 70 years.[48]

[45] Provided by State of Queensland (Department of Transport and Main Roads) *December 1983, Queensland roads : official journal of the Main Roads Department, Queensland.* 13.

[46] O'Connor, Colin. *Bridging two centuries - Historic bridges of Australia.* (St Lucia: University of Queensland Press, 1985) 174.

[47] O'Connor, Colin. *Bridging two centuries - Historic bridges of Australia.* (St Lucia: University of Queensland Press, 1985) 175.

[48] Provided by State of Queensland (Department of Transport and Main Roads) 1947, *Twenty-sixth annual report of the*

Both of these bridges had very good service lives accommodating dramatic changes in the traffic they carried. A custom designed bridge incorporating best practice would last much longer.

Commissioner of Main Roads for year ended 30th June, 1947. 8.

8. Truss Bridges

Fig. 72. Timber truss at Ravenshoe, Queensland, 1920.

The necessity of rapidly expanding colonies after the discovery of gold and the need for Public Works Departments to build infrastructure as cheaply as possible using materials that were at hand, saw many timber truss bridges constructed. Between 1861 and 1936, New South Wales built 407 timber truss bridges, all to unique Australian designs, and by 2013, there were still 48 being maintained by their Roads and Marine Service (RMS formerly the RTA).[49]

---

[49] Australian Society for History of Engineering and Technology. *Timber Trussed Bridges of NSW*. January 2013. URL: http://ashet.org.au/timber-truss-bridges/. Date visited. September 7, 2015. In 1992 there were 81 trusses in NSW. Because these bridges were expected to be replaced in the short term, maintenance was run down allowing the bridges to deteriorate prior to the commitment to preserve them. Lau, Benjamin. Repairs and Strengthening of Timber Bridge Trusses in *Proceedings of 1992 Timber Bridges Conference* 232.

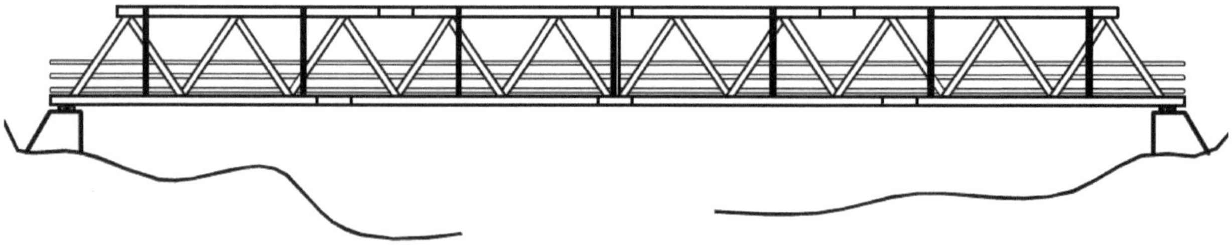

Fig. 73. Preliminary drawing of our first truss bridge.[50]

In about 1986, we wanted to add a truss to our range so our old engineer, before he had blotted his copybook with the bridge mentioned in the Background section, prepared basic engineering for a 31 m truss for us. The sizes were later confirmed for us by an engineer we trusted. The sizes included 250x125 mm for top and bottom cords and 200x150 mm for transoms. These sizes are probably not a great deal smaller than would have been used in the vehicle bridges. Back then, the log supply would have allowed us to produce the timber but with some difficulty. That is not the case now. The RMS plans to only maintain and keep in use 25 of their remaining bridges and these will be representative samples spread over the whole state. This reduced number was driven by the difficulty in obtaining sufficient large section timber of durable species. The logs required are rare outside of national parks. [51] So, for Australian designers at least, we can discount large timber trusses using sawn members as a viable option for a new bridge. Laminated beams are an alternate replacement material but refer the special requirements of this material in the next chapter.

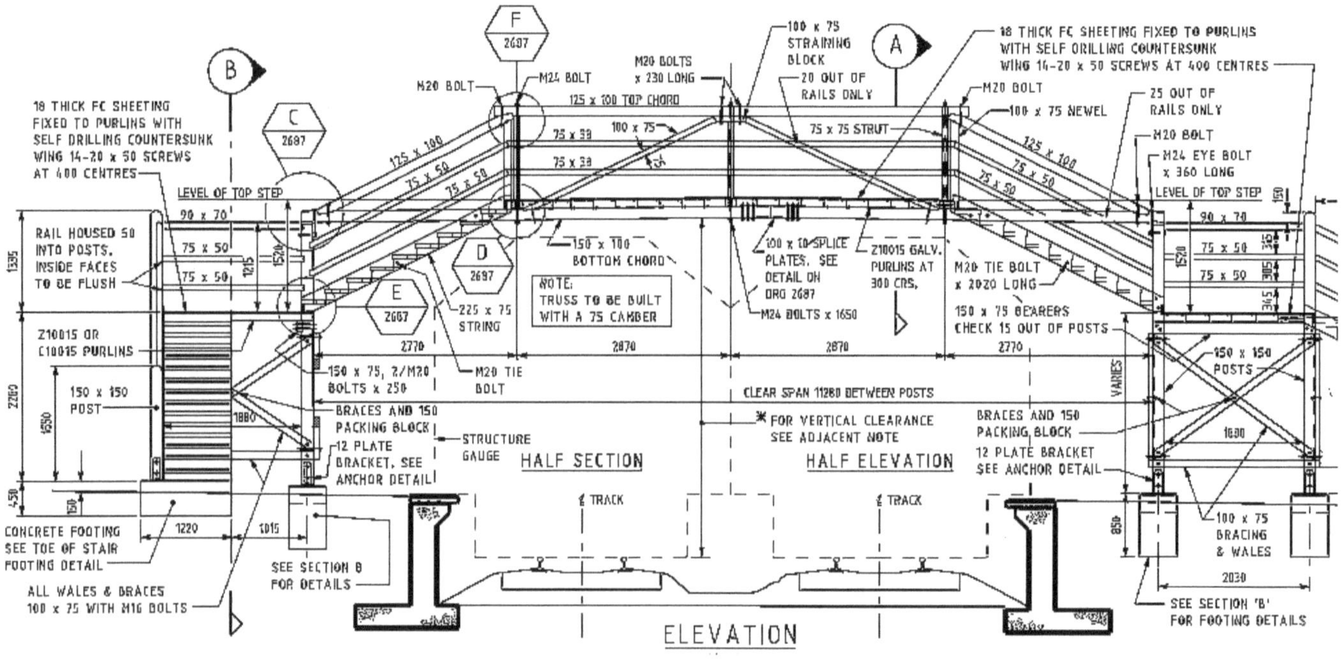

Fig. 74. Queensland Rail truss bridge.

---

[50] Consider as representative only as codes would have changes since first drawn.
[51] Road and Traffic Authority. *Timber truss road bridges - A strategic approach to conservation, July 2011* 16 URL: http://www.rms.nsw.gov.au/documents/projects/key-build-programs/maintenance/timber-truss-road-bridges/timber-truss-road-bridges-report-july11.pdf. Date accessed: September 7, 2015.

For shorter spans, sawn timber trusses with bolted connections have made viable footbridges. Figure Seventy-four shows a typical Queensland Rail design for an 11.28 metre span. While it could be argued that this design no longer suits the needs of a modern rail system e.g. impact resistance of the piers, the load carrying ability of this design when maintained is proven – refer Figure Thirty-five. I have seen old plans for this bridge for spans up to 52 feet span or about 16 metres. The bridge in Figure Thirty-five was a replacement in 2002 of an earlier bridge of similar design in my home town. The earlier bridge was already old when I was a boy and it performed well with not a great deal of maintenance. Unfortunately, the timber species selection for the replacement bridge was not as good as with the original. The species is not nominated and the grade is only F17.

Every truss mentioned so far has a critical weakness. That is, the vertical bolts through the top cord. At a conference in 1992, I heard that, as part of the maintenance of the historic timber bridges, the RTA was trialing a metal roof on top of the trusses.[52] I thought, that was obvious, why did it take 100 years to think about that? Then in 2011 at another conference, I heard a bridge maintenance specialist say that this had created a microclimate under the iron that actually promoted decay even further! But there were other problems as well. It was a traditional to paint timber members as this was thought to be an effective barrier to moisture, which it is if it is perfectly maintained. But this didn't happen and, when the paint cracked, water penetrated and sat under the paint providing a perfect environment for fungal growth. This was particularly a problem with the top cord. The historical bridges also suffered decay at the splice and the truss panel points. That is, everywhere there was a bolt. The other problem area was the timber to timber interfaces, especially where there was horizontal contact.[53]

Many of these problems could have been very easily reduced substantially at the design stage by taking basic measures to enhance durability. For example, shaping the top and bottom chord to shed moisture away from the joints. Utilising some of the hardware shown in Figure Fifty-six to retreat the joints would also assist. Painting large dimension timbers is problematic as it seals in moisture and prevents the wood from breathing and drying so they would probably have been better unpainted or at least treated with CN Oil.[54] All these problems could have been all but eliminated with a roof.

We did have a plan for a truss using realistic sizes, if I recall correctly, mainly 150x50 mm and with everything connected with split rings. But before we could build our first bridge to this design our consultant rang us to tell us that the design was no longer valid. He advised that, after a failure, the design value of the split rings was reduced to a third for external work.[55] This highlights the problem with lighter trussed bridges. How do you develop a strong connection with small timber sizes that will withstand the elements for over 50 years? As was discussed in the chapter on fasteners, it is impractical with nailplates. They are not further discussed in this chapter as I do not see them as a viable option.

---

[52] Lau. *Repairs …*, 237.

[53] Lau. *Repairs …,* 233-4.

[54] Tingley, Dan. *Pers. Com.* September 7, 2015. If paint is used, Dr Tingley advises that it should have less than 30% solids.

[55] The exact details are not known but it was recalled this way, "At one time split rings and shear plates were downgraded because of a failure and the distance from the ends of the member were increased especially for tension members. Additionally the strength was downgraded if there was a moisture problem i.e. weather exposure, swimming pools etc." Pierce, James. *Pers. Com.* September 9, 2015.

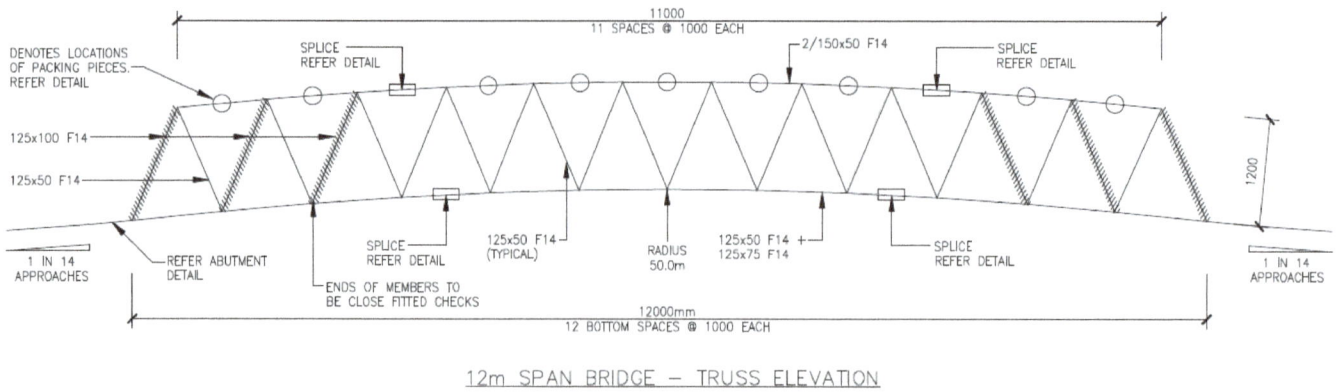

Fig. 75. Truss based on Scottish Countryside Commission design.

Fig. 76. The prototype truss

The Countryside Commission of Scotland had developed an attractive curved truss which we used as inspiration for a new truss bridge. Heavy (i.e. expensive) galvanised brackets replaced nailplates so we had excellent connections at the nodes. By putting the decking on the diagonal we did not have to brace between the two trusses giving excellent lateral stability. Overall, it proved difficult to curve the 125x75 mm bottom rail so making the bridge labour intensive as one-offs and to have made these on an ongoing commercial basis would have required expensive jigs to curve the timber and reduce labour costs. That, coupled with cost of the brackets, made the bridge commercially unviable against the light nailplated pine trusses. For all that, it is a design that was worthy of development.[56] The drawing in Figure Seventy-five should only be considered indicative. While it is a vast improvement on the nailplated bridge, it does not have a roof. In our climate even the most durable timber will eventually succumb as will steel.

---

[56] Contact the author for more information.

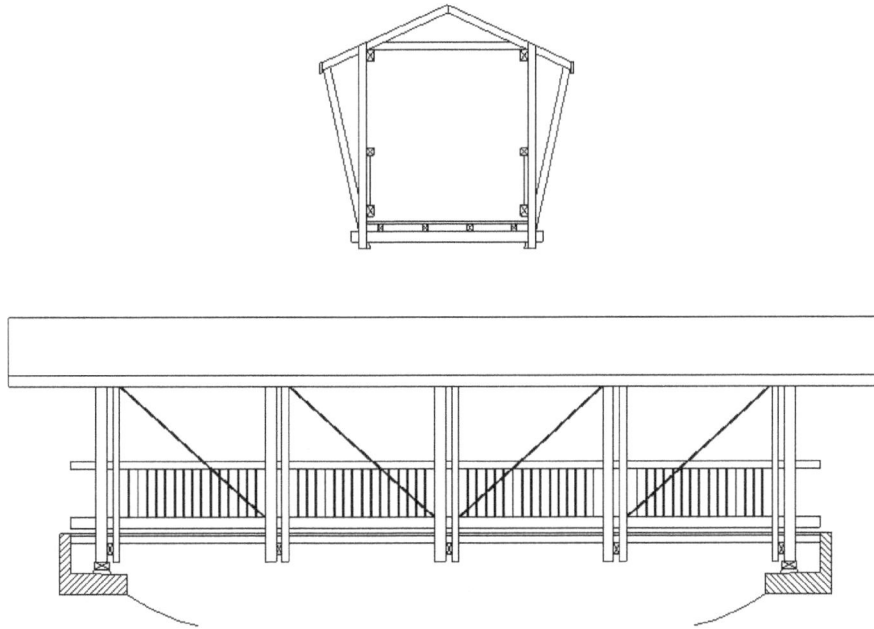

Fig. 77 Concept for a covered timber bridge.

For Australian conditions, timber trusses should be roofed and Figure Seventy-seven is another concept that is worth exploring. It draws inspiration from the covered bridge at Wimmis in Switzerland.

9. Laminated Beam Bridges

Fig. 78. Laminated beam being delivered in Germany

Laminated beams should be the ideal material for constructing footbridges. They are light compared to steel and log girders and can be manufactured to any size that may be required. The only consideration as far as size is concerned is transport and the limitations imposed by the size of the presses at the fabrication plant. Laminated bridges are also far easier to build than log bridges because the carpenters do not have to deal with irregular and tapered members. But, when I explored the economics, they were not an option for the shorter spans that I was building with logs. In these cases the laminated beams themselves are much more expensive and the detailing required is also more expensive. This was not the case with very long span bridges and here they have the potential to excel over alternatives.

Fig. 79. Arched Laminated Bridge.

Fig. 80. Delamination of arched bridge.

The glues that have traditionally been used in Laminated beams are very effective when used internally and the bond is stronger than the timber it is gluing. Used internally these beams are trouble free but not so when used externally. The problem with laminated timber bridges in our Queensland conditions is that the timber delaminates due to the effect of wetting and drying and UV. Usually it is the timber itself which fails beside the glueline, not the glueline itself. Further compounding matters are the deck fasteners which can be screwed directly into the girders which causes deterioration of the beam itself. The effect is much less in colder climates but, it is not that the deterioration does not occur, it just takes longer.

Fig. 81. Untreated pine heartwood.

Softwoods are used more often in laminated beam bridges as they glue far more easily than hardwood. The pine also costs much less than hardwood to produce. But there is a downside as well. It is well known that the heartwood of hardwood cannot be treated but this is no concern if a species with the correct natural durability is chosen. It is less well known that the heart of pine is just as untreatable but it is not durable. Every laminate in a beam of standard construction has to be selected carefully so as not to contain heartwood.

Fig. 82. Procting the beam.   **Fig. 83** Separate fastening beams.

Our consultant developed a laminated beam bridge for us that worked around the limitations of the standard laminated beam. The beam itself was made from pine with the individual laminates LOSP) treated prior to laminating. This is very important as it is possible to purchase lower price beams that are treated after glueing. The preservative effect would have been more effective had the beams been painted with CN (copper napthenate) oil as well. The outer beam is shielded with a set of timber louvres (Figure Eighty-two) that protects from the rain and the UV. Using the maximum possible overhang on the decking also helps. The decking was not fastened directly into the beams. Figure Eighty-three shows the use of ex 100x100 bolting rails that are fastened to the sides of the beams These rails have a sloping top to direct rainwater away from the beam. This particular bridge was designed for a small fire truck to cross as well as pedestrians so it required heavy 70 mm decking and was bolted from the top.

Fig. 84. Fastening rail for decking.

For a pedestrian bridge, not in a marine situation, a hot dipped galvanised angle fastened to the beams would be used allowing the decking to be fastened from underneath as on this trussed bridge. In a coastal situation 304 grade stainless would be substituted. The rail is about 6 mm under the top of the beam and so, when the decking is screwed there is some flexing of the rail, which keeps the unseasoned decking tight on the beams. Spacing the rail away from the beams (say 6 mm) assists with durability also.

Fig. 85. Stiffeners.

Fig. 86 Flashings.

In this design the beams would be stiffened by inserting a number of diaphragms, we would use laminated beam for this as well but steel could equally be used. Our practice was to protect the tops of the beams and the diaphragms with aluminium flashings. With heavier decking, moisture is deflected off the top of the beam onto the bolting rail and due to its taper is quickly shed from the structure. This decking would only be fastened at the centre and edges requiring the centre beams to be installed higher (otherwise termed hogged) so that some pre-tensioning is placed on the decking which assists in compensating for seasoning i.e. shrinkage and so reduce rattling of the deck.

Fig. 87. Pedestrian bridge delaminating (note galvanised bands around the beam).

The effort that went into this ensuring this bridge would achieve a long trouble free life is more than would normally be encountered.[57] Even with this level of care we refused to sell this bridge above Rockhampton i.e. in the wet tropics. Fundamentally, our opinion was that the standard laminated beam was unsuited for bridge construction. Preservatives could deal with decay but wetting and drying would still make the beam delaminate. The bridge in Figure Eighty-seven which is delaminating badly is in one of the cooler southern states. There is not even lip service to good design principles for standard beams.

---

[57] The detailing of the bridge described meets the requirements outlined in Hyne's Technical Data Sheet 6 URL: http://www.hyne.com.au/downloads/technical_info/TDS_6_MAY14_FINAL_WEB.pdf. Date Visited 4 September 2015

Fig. 88. Incised timber.

Fig. 89. Beam using cyclic delamination resistant glues.

This situation is changing at the time of writing. Glues have now been developed that are cyclic delamination resistant. These are critical for resisting the constant wetting and drying that can be encountered. The difficulty in effectively treating pine can be overcome by using material that is incised. Incising is a process, relatively uncommon in Australia where incisions are made in the timber creating pockets in otherwise untreatable timber which allows the treatments to penetrate. Incising allows the beam plant to assemble, cut to length and fully pre-drill the beam prior to treatment. This is a great advantage. This can be followed with an additional fire retardant treatment. I am not aware of any manufacturers of this style of beam in Australia but they are being imported to Australia from the USA. There is still a reluctance to embrace this type of construction in Australia as there is overseas but some bridges are starting to be installed.

Fig. 90. 120 metre clear span laminated beam bridge.[58]

---

[58] This timber bridge was developed for OSA by Timber Restoration Systems.

It is expected that initial reluctance to large timber structures will slowly be overcome.

Curved Bridges

Curved bridges are visually far more attractive than those using straight girders. As laminated beams are easily made with a curve they lend themselves to this type of bridge. All curved bridges are often incorrectly called *arched bridges* by the public and often by engineers. An arched bridge is one where the loads are transmitted into the ground horizontally as in the bridge pictured in Figure Ninety-one. In reality the forces are so great in an arched bridge that it is unusual to find a site that is suited to their use. True arched bridges will normally need massive concrete abutments that make their use very costly. Generally what will be sold is a simply supported girder that happens to be curved.

Fig. 91. The rise in this bridge is too high.

The maximum rise for a bridge is 1 in 8. That does not mean that if the bridge is eight metres long the rise in the centre is one metre. The measurement is taken from a tangent at the beginning of the bridge where the rise is steeper. Figure Ninety-one clearly shows how this rise is not equal over the length. The introduction of stairs into a public structure like the bridge in Figures Seventy-nine and Ninety-one which was built before the requirements of the disability code, would be unthinkable now.

Fig. 92. One in eight radial rise.

The *Building Code of Australia* refers to a rise of only 1 in 14. When applied radially, this would result in a very small rise in the centre and would be of minimal aesthetic value. The bridge on the right has a radial rise of 1 in 8. While larger curves can easily be accommodated they should not be considered unless the client has specifically nominated and is informed of non-compliance to either the bridge or disability code. I have seen bridges on golf courses where a higher rise is appropriate.

10. Barriers

Some Terminology

Before starting my discussion of barriers, the terminology I am using for the individual components needs to be defined. For forty years I was supplying builders with dressed breadloaf shaped 70x70 mm which all my builders all called handrail and 65x19 mm which they all called balustrade. Fit it all together with a bottom rail and it was called "the handrail" and the supplier, builder and homeowner knew what was meant. Terminology from the standards, codes and technical data sheets, in my mind, confuses what was once simple. Now different professionals and trades people can understand different things by the same terminology. Refer Appendix C for the myriad of terms used. My terminology, which is a mixture of codes and common usage, is as follows

Railings – the collective term for posts, rails and balusters – used in the bridge code
Top rail – the uppermost rail in a set of railings
Bottom rail – the lowest rail in a set of railings
Mid rail – any intermediate rail
Balustrade – a series of balusters
Handrail – a lower "grab" rail that is offset from the main railings for disabled compliance
Bikeway rail – a high rail offset from the main railings for bikeway compliance

Fig. 93. Millenium Bridge, London.

Fig. 94. Southgate bridge, Melbourne.

The Elephant in the Room

There is an elephant in the room when it comes to any discussion of bridge railings, and that is, that the code is probably incorrect, or perhaps better worded as, too inflexible. Consider Figures Ninety-three and Ninety-four. The Millennium Bridge in London was designed by some of the sharpest minds in that country and the Southgate Bridge in Melbourne has won awards for engineering. People who are that accomplished in their profession generally do not make basic mistakes yet both of these bridges have horizontal wire balustrades. This is surprising as the Australian bridge code only allows vertical balustrade, (granted the UK code may be different but the risk is the same). Even a cursory look at Australian kit footbridges is enough to realise that there is a considerable amount of freedom used in the design of footbridge railings.

The difficulty for designers is that there is no standalone code for footbridges. They are all part of AS 5100 *Bridge Design Code* and there, a footbridge is conceived as being part of a high level road bridge from which a fall would unquestioningly be fatal. Most footbridges are better termed "park bridges" with relatively low fall heights. A more reasonable expectation (and this seems to be the case with both these bridges, by both designers and judges) is to apply the geometry of the Building Code of Australia while adopting the load and deflection requirements of the Bridge Design Code. That will be the approach taken in this chapter and will only see vertical balustrade being required in areas where the fall height is in excess of 4.0

Fig. 95. Railings that meets no codes.

m. While I question one standard's suitability, that is not the same thing as abandoning codes altogether as with Figure Ninety-five.

When do you Need a Railing?

Fig. 96. Swale drain without railing.

Fig. 97. Bikeway rail with low fall height.

In Figures Ninety-six and Ninety-seven we have decks with similar fall heights and a both fall onto grass, but one has a kerb, the other has a partial barrier with the required bikeway rail. If we use the BCA as the guide for when we install a railing, it is only mandated after the fall height reaches 1000 mm so there was no railing used on the swale drain bridge. The partial barrier is used on the bikeway because it is required when the fall height is only 250 mm, meaning there will be no bridge which is classed as a bikeway that will not require a railing, and not just any railing, it must be bikeway compliant. It is claimed that it is more dangerous to have a railing that is non compliant than to have no railing at all.[59]

There are times when it is uncertain if and what standards apply. Is the swale drain crossing in Figure Ninety-six a bridge or just a single span boardwalk? A full discussion of codes that might apply in a number of situations and recommendations is found in my *Boardwalk Design Guide*. It is always wise for a risk assessment to be carried out for the whole project by the asset owner and for guidance to

---

[59] Austroads. *Guide to traffic Engineering Practice*, (Sydney: Austroads 1999). 113.

be given to the designer. We have found over the years that there is no uniformity in expectation.

A Tip from the Author: We supplied some swale bridges to a project where they were sited over a gently flowing small creek. The fall height was under a metre and all was well until it rained just before final inspection. There was about 200 mm of scouring and an order was put on the developer to install railings. If there is likelihood of scouring I suggest that you work on 800 mm instead of 1000 mm as your start point for installing a railing.

Railing Geometry

Fig. 98. Combined "bikeway" and disabled access.

What should be a simple matter can be unnecessarily complicated. We designed a level timber walkway to a railway station which had to be bikeway compliant (refer Figure Ninety-eight). This was achieved by having the top rail offset 150 mm on a sloping steel post. Then the project architect decided that she wanted to add a disabled compliant handrail as well. Our consultant protested, "You can't have both. The required geometry for a bikeway is incompatible with the disabled geometry." There is a danger that you can hit your pedals on the disabled kerb and the code of practice for bikeways clearly says it is dangerous to have non compliant geometry. The agreed outcome was that the path would be signposted, "Cyclists dismount". The sign was not installed by the builder making it a legal nightmare if there is an accident. There is a real need for those who sit on different standards dealing with railings to talk to each other and determine a geometry that is acceptable for all bridge applications. At the time of writing this is not the situation we have to deal with.

Because of the difficulty in combining the disabled and the cycleway requirements we try very hard to ensure the bridge will go in level or at the most under a 1 in 33 slope (confirm). This removes the necessity of installing a disabled compliant handrail and you are dealing with much more clearly defined railing requirements.

We developed a number of bridge railings when I was operating Outdoor Structures Australia and I share them with you as a guide as you seek to develop the railings with the aesthetics needed for your project.

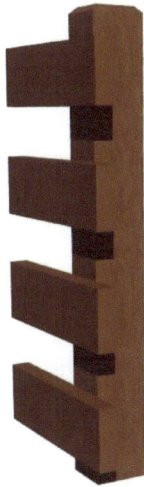

Fig. 99. Pedestrian railing system P1 (Lockyer) system. Top rail at 1020 mm.

Fig. 100. Pedestrian railing systems P2 and P3 (Lockyer with grabrail) Top rail at 1020 and 1110 mm respectively

Fig. 101. Pedestrian railing systems P4 and P5 (Queenslander with grabrail). Top rail at 1020 and 1110 mm respectively

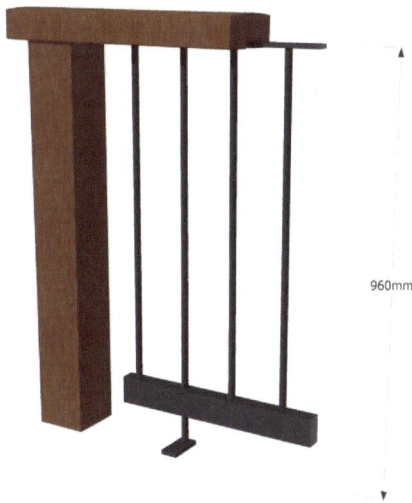

Fig. 102. Pedestrian railing system P6 and P7 Carr style. Top rail height varies with profile. Panel is 960 and 1060 mm high respectively.

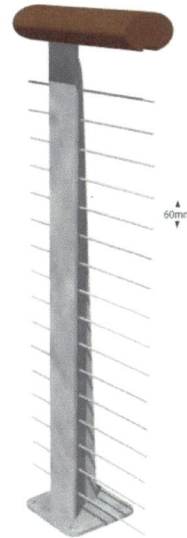

Fig 103. Barrier System P8 (Cruiseliner style). Top rail height varies with profile

Figures Ninety-nine to One hundred and three which show systems P1 to P8 are all for pedestrian use. The codes that they meet and the fall heights are listed in Table Four below.

Mark	Style	BCA	Bridge	Tracks	Bicycle
P1	Lockyer Standard	Fall heights to 4.0 m	N/A	Type B	N/A
P2	Lockyer + Grabrail	Fall heights to 4.0 m	N/A	Type B	N/A
P3	Lockyer + Grabrail	Fall heights to 4.0 m	N/A	Type B	N/A
P4	Queenslander + grabrail	All fall heights	N/A	Type A	N/A
P5	Queenslander + grabrail	All fall heights	All fall heights	Type A	N/A
P6	Carr – Low	All fall heights	N/A	Type A	N/A
P7	Carr - High	All fall heights	All fall heights	Type A	N/A
P8	Cruiserliner	Fall heights to 4.0 m	N/A	Type B	N/A
Table 4. Code compliance and fall height of different pedestrian railing systems.					

For bikeway rails we developed the following.

Fig. 104. Bikeway system C1 (partial barrier) system. Top rail at 1300 mm.

Fig. 105. Typical bikeway termination.

Fig. 106. Baikeway system C2 (Lockyer) system. Top rail at 1300 mm.

Fig. 107. Baikeway system C3 (Queenslander). Toprail at 1300 mm.

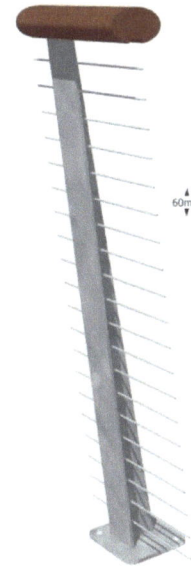

Fig. 108. Baikeway system C4 (Cruiseliner bikerail). Toprail at 1300 mm.

Figures 104 to 105 which show systems C1 to C4 are bikeway use. The codes that they meet and the fall heights are listed in Table Five below.

Mark	Style	BCA	Bridge	Tracks	Bicycle
C1	Partial rail	Fall heights to 1.0 m	N/A	Type D	Fall Heights to 2.0 m
C2	Lockyer + Cyclerail	Fall heights to 4.0 m	N/A	Type B	Fall Heights to 2.0 m
C3	Queenslander + Cyclerail	All fall heights	All fall heights	Type A	All fall heights
C4*	Cruiserliner + cyclerail	Fall heights to 4.0 m	N/A	Type B	Fall Heights to 2.0 m
E.g. A mixed use boardwalk to comply with both the Cycle Code and the BCA can only use a C1 system when the fall height is less than 1.0m					
*The extra height, the inclined arrangement, the wide top and the narrowness of the wires does not make it easy for a child to climb					
Table 5. Code compliance and fall height of different bikeway railing systems.					

For a more complete discussion of railing geometry refer to my *Commercial Barrier Guide.*

Railing Aesthetics

Fig. 109. Four bridges with totally different aesthetics.

For most bridges, the aesthetics is almost all in the railings. The four bridges in Figure 109 look totally different and set the tone for the locality in which they are set[60]. Closer inspection shows the railings are simply bolted on to a girder and deck which is essentially the same in all applications. While it is simple to order from a catalogue which has a few standard designs to choose from, it must be remembered that the railings should be more than meeting basic dimensions and geometry. Railings should also be architecture. A relatively small investment in an attractive railing gives a large return, lifting the ordinary to the extraordinary. Footbridges do not have to be minimalist.

---

[60] Notice that none of these bridges meet the bridge code but also the fall height is under 4.2m

Railing Engineering

Because the deflection requirements for railings are so demanding, they can be the most difficult part of the bridge to design. Earlier versions of the bridge code had deflection requirements for the rails but not for the balustrade. Despite that, prudent designers always made these sufficiently robust to minimise vandalism and, in steel, this virtually dictated a 16 mm bar and I have often seen 20 mm used. The later editions now nominate a deflection limit for the balustrade as well. The requirements are that a 0.75 kN load should not deflect the rail or the balustrade by more than 1 in 800. After including a load factor of 1.5, this means that a load of 112 kg should not deflect the top and bottom rail with supports at 2400 mm by more than 3 mm and a 1000 mm baluster by more than 1.25 mm. Figure 110 shows a case where the designer has taken the easy route and used standard pool fencing instead of a designing a compliant bridge rail. After all, the balustrades are vertical and the gaps are right. Notice that two bars are broken out completely and others are bent. The economy of a light rail is not matched by the cost of litigation that results should a child fall through the gap.

Fig. 110. Pool fencing used as bridge railing.

Timber Quality

Timber quality is dealt with on the chapter on timber for footbridges.

Fig. 111. Queenslander P4 railing system with handrail.

Fig. 112 Handrail from covered bridge at Sandgate.

Good Detailing on Railings

Fig. 113. Replacement top rail on Thames Embankment.

Back in 2005 I was walking along the Thames embankment near the London Eye when I spotted some top rail that was being replaced. It was originally installed in 1953 for the Queen's coronation. So that is a service life of 52 years. The original top rail had a very neat splice and was being replaced in the same way (Figure 113). This splice held moisture and it eventually decayed at these joins. Beyond the splice, the timber was almost as good as the day it was installed. I realised then that even if a long life is achieved, the acceptable service life to an asset owner for a timber railing is always going to be 10 years longer than was actually achieved.

Fig. 114. Top rail after 30 years in Gatton, Queensland.

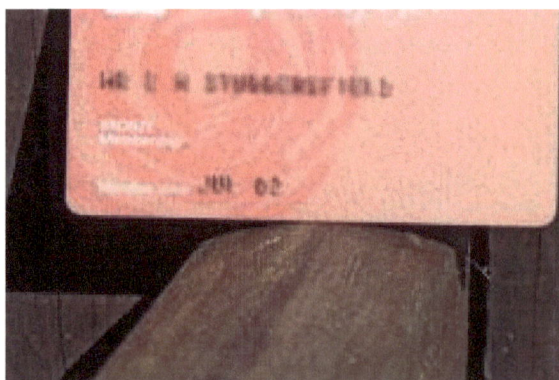

Fig. 115. Moisture shedding rail.

One of the first bridges I ever supplied was back in 1986 to a park opposite my home. I had been watching the bridge closely over the years and I noticed that the tops of 45 mm wide rails eventually started to show signs of degrade. Figure 114 is typical of the degrade that occurred after 29 years but some areas had more degrade. (The rails were actually replaced a week after the image was taken but could have just been rolled over and put the protected edge upwards). Observing this degrade led me to change the design of our rails so that they all shed moisture, refer Figure 115 for an example of an ex 50 mm vertical rail.

Fig. 116. Diagonally aligned top rail on heritage listed fence.

Fig. 117. Footbridge with diagonally aligned top rail.

Of course, the most effective water shedding railing is when the top rail is mounted on the diagonal. The image on the left is from a heritage listed cricket ground at the Gatton campus of the University of Queensland. The image was taken in 2014 just before it was replaced. Some rails had failed but most are still sound. It should have probably been replaced ten years earlier. I have another image of the same fence in 1940 but do not know how old it was then. This gives a useful life of at least 65 years. Detailing to shed moisture will reward you.

Attaching the Top Rail to the Post

Fig. 118. Top rail in Canberra fastened from underneath.

Fig. 119. Same structure where the top rail was extended and fastened from the top.

Fig. 120. Decay at top rail join.

As for the need for fastening from underneath, Figure 119 clearly illustrates the shortcomings of top fixing. The main part of the top rail in that structure is fastened from underneath using galvanised brackets and is in good order despite having some age. An extension which was top fixed has failed. It is not hard to fix from underneath and, like a moisture shedding profile, well worth the extra effort involved.

The top rail in the same structure is flat and is not shedding moisture quickly. This is allowing any moisture to more readily go down the join and enter through the end grain (which can absorb moisture 8 times faster than through the face) and cause decay at the ends. There should be at least 6 mm end clearance between the rails to prevent moisture being held by capillary action but, this constitutes a possible finger entrapment. A strap over the join was the old way of protecting the join from moisture and is still good practice (see Figure 116). The strap prevents finger entrapment as well if a gap is introduced.

Spans

Fig. 121. Each top rail has taken a set downwards.

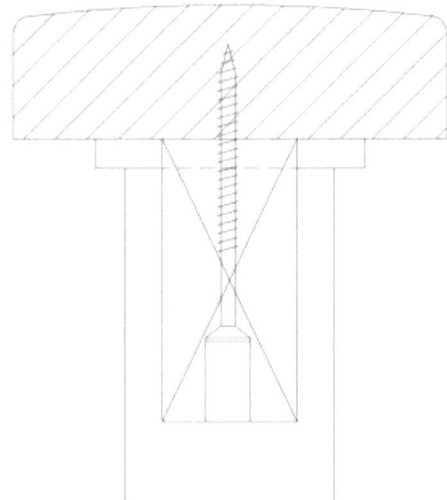

Fig. 122. Later versions use a multiple span with a stiffener underneath.

A few years ago, I drove past one of my early boardwalks and, even from a distance, I was reminded that I could have done a much better job. The boardwalk was certified and remains structurally sound. My failure was, at that time, to not understand the characteristics of timber. I did not appreciate how simple spans affected top rail aesthetics. The condition of the top rail timber was excellent; it was just that every piece had taken a set downwards. This was despite the top rail being ex 125x100 mm with a water shedding profile, and the span only 2400 mm! This unfortunate situation occurred soon after the boardwalk was completed. When I look at the image above and reflect on what my eye saw on site, it appeared much worse on location. The visual effect is compounded as it is an unbroken line and eye tends to magnify the effect of the set.

After first seeing what had happened, we changed the way we design and supply our top rails for that particular boardwalk. Instead of the original heavy size which is expensive and difficult to produce in long lengths, we would now use our horizontal top rail (ex 150x50 mm) with a domed top extending over two spans. We would then secure a 100x50 mm on edge underneath as a stiffener. This has proved stable. Whatever design option you choose, the important thing is to not have simple spans. Instead, support the top rail over three posts as mentioned. We would use 2000 mm as the normal post spacing for larger size rails as this means that a multiple span can be sourced from a readily available[61] 4200 mm length. As invariably happens, the run is not a multiple of

Fig. 123. Breaking the line of sight with a post.

4000 mm and if needed you can source a single 6000 mm length to finish without too many problems. Alternatively, a centre prop can be used if lengths are single span, (refer to the Case History, Cairns marina).

Attaching the Post to the Girder.

The complication in attaching the post to the bridge is shrinkage. If say you use a 100 mm thick unseasoned beam and a 125x125 mm post the total thickness is 225 mm. If you have specified a lower shrinkage timber like spotted gum with 6% movement you have to deal with 13-14 mm of shrinkage. It will also take about 4-5 years for the timber to stabilise. You really don't want to return initially after six months and then annually for the next four years to tighten the nuts. Don't specify kiln dried as you cannot commercially dry anything beyond 50 mm thick[62] and recycled is likely to behave just like green off saw timber.

Fig. 124. Volute Washer.

Fig. 125. Volute washer on post.

As was mentioned, a product that has long been used in the power industry for pole hardware that is impractical to retighten is a volute washer[63]. These stainless steel coils can take up 25 mm of shrinkage

---

[61] Readily available, that is, in sizes such as 150x50 mm, not readily available in 125x100 mm which has to be very straight to pass through the planer.

[62] This fact is not widely recognised and I constantly see drawings where sizes of 150x150 mm and 200x200 mm are specified as kiln dried.

[63] The volute washer is a coil of approximately 6 mm stainless spring steel wire that compresses within itself. It is available in a range of sizes to suit 12, 16, 20 and 24 mm bolts. The volute washer needs a square washer under the nut. When we use

without the need to ever retighten. These should be an integral part of any railing post attachment. Figure 125 shows its application on a post. A square washer is required under the nut and, if going against a painted surface, our practice is to use a square washer underneath as well.

Ideally the post should be separated from the girder by a spacer about 6 mm thick. This will minimise the contact between the two members and reduce the likelihood of moisture being retained.

Other Matters
Frangible Railings

Fig. 126. Frangible pine rails.

Fig. 127. Frangible Hardwood rails.

The railings frequently fill with debris during floods and so become a solid wall which can impose so great a load that the whole structure is at risk. Because of this, some bridges are fitted with a frangible rail which can be either completely sacrificial or fold over under load. But generally speaking, railings are not meant to fail. Instead, people expect them to be safe and to be able to take a very large impact The railing in Figure 126 is effectively one piece of 90x35 mm MGP12 or 14 treated pine used in a place where you would expect a minimum of 100x100 mm hardwood. This post may conceivably break from pedestrian impact. The post in Figure 127 is 100x100 mm with a saw cut 10 mm deep. It is designed to take a large pedestrian impact and to only break away under a severe flood event.

It is my opinion that frangible railings should be approached with great caution and only used as a last resort when other reasonable engineering options fail. If they are adopted pedestrian safety is foremost over protection of the bridge.

---

them on a painted surface we use a large square washer under the volute washer itself to prevent damage to the paint. With the brand we use, the m12/16 washer measures approx. 65 mm across and about 30 mm high and the m20/24 washer measures 85x35 mm. Remember that you need longer bolts. In the image the washer is not fully tightened so it can be seen.

Kerb Design

Fig 128. Do not trap moisture under a kerb

When the fall height is under 1.0 m, under the Building Code of Australia there is no requirement to have a handrail but normal practice is to add a kerb mainly to assist with restraining wheelchairs. When disability code compliance is required a kerb is also added.

When the kerb is bolted directly to the deck it traps moisture and prevents the deck from being self-cleaning. The board under the kerb in ?? has decayed under the kerb. The requirements of the disability code so as not to foul the kickplates of a wheelchair will be met by spacing a 75 mm thick kerb off the deck by 75 mm.

Railing Height with Horses

Fig. 129. Trooper McKay on Yahoo.

Over the years, I have often been asked how high a railing should be on a footbridge to suit horses. When I say 1800 mm, people always look at me askance and then ask if I have engineering for our decking for horse loads. But I did meet someone who wanted a footbridge on a horse trail. Without asking my advice she told me the rail must be 1800 mm high. The difference was that she rode a horse. The railing height is as important as the decking size.

Authors Note: The bridge in the image is the one mentioned in *Good Detailing of Railings* above. It was supplied by me back in 1986 to the park opposite my house and up to 2015 had received no maintenance other than have two deck boards replaced. After 26 years, when the image was taken, it still easily accommodates a horse and rider but the decking was replaced not long after the image was taken. The degradation of the surface fibres made it look as if it needed replacing.

Which is Better, Timber or Steel?

Fig. 130. Warren truss built by the author with galvanised steel railings.

Fig. 131. Warren truss built by the author with painted timber railings.

Two versions of my Warren truss bridge are shown in Figures 130 and 131. There is a large price difference between the two options. In a 20x2.5 m bridge, at the time of writing, the bridge with the steel rails is roughly a 25% dearer than the timber version. These steel rails are designed to the bridge code, not the swimming pool fence requirements. So, considering the extra expense, are the steel rails the low maintenance option?

One exasperated council engineer explained to me that he would rather see timber than steel on his employer's footbridges. His problem was that the contractors would take their mowers over the bridges and frequently snagged the mower on the balustrade. With steel, the panel would have to be removed and usually a new one copied. While this was happening, the bridge would be taken out of service. The repair was costly and time consuming. But, with timber, he could send a carpenter out and have the same damage repaired for nominal cost and in a very short time. So the practicalities make timber a very reasonable choice.

Authors Note: Painting bridge railings has its own problems. Refer to the chapter Leaching and Finishing in my book, *Architectural Timber Battens*.

Stainless Wires

Fig. 132. Badly designed wire rope termination.

The tension imposed on the post and fasteners can be massive, Consider a railing with the posts at 2.0 m rigged with 4 mm, 7x19 stainless wire. At the time of writing the BCA required the individual wires to be tensioned to 1.075 kN. A railing at 1 m high needs 15 wires, so imposing a total load of over 16 kN to the posts and fastenings. At 80 mm spacings (with a centre support) this is still eleven wires and a load of over 10 kN. Because of this it is prudent to fit solid blocking between the posts as shown in Figure 133.

Stainless wires are frequently used in conjunction with timber top rail and they are not always done well as Figure 132 illustrates. There the wires terminate at eyed coachscrews in conjunction with inexpensive commodity grade fittings which have failed.

It is necessary to specify every item in the rope system and give close attention to the termination. There is a big difference between the systems. The one we normally use will span 20 m between terminations, others can be half that distance. Not all have the warranty you need for public use.

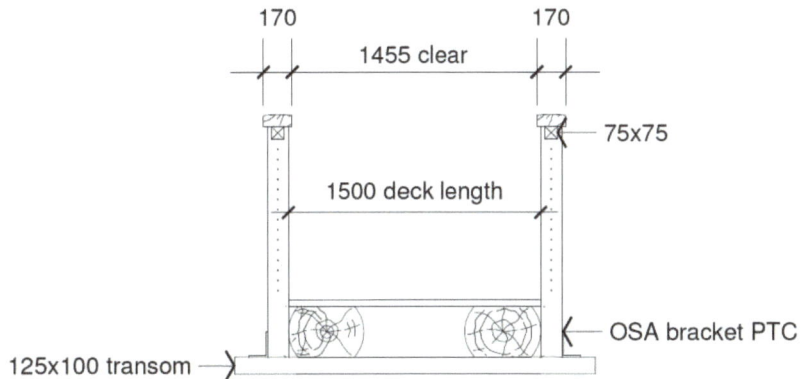

Fig. 133. 75x75 blocking in-between the posts.

There is a complete discussion of stainless wires in railings in my *Commercial Barrier Guide.*

Railing Case History

Cairns Port Authority Marina.

Figure 134 shows railings at the Port of Cairns Authority marina. It is probably the best railings I have seen and it is not one of mine! The top rail itself has a good slope on it to shed moisture and, equally important, there is a significant gap between each piece so no moisture is held at the join and a finger trap is avoided. Fastening is from underneath. A small centre support is enough to hold the rail from taking a set either up or down.

Fig. 134. Boardwalk railings at Cairns Marina.

Boardwalk in Queensland

Fig. 135. Not one thing about this post is right..

This image shows how not to design, supply and construct a bridge railing. Consider the six failures in this item.

1. Timber Quality. The post has a large loose gum vein that has opened up along the length. This is a piece that should have been supplied as exposed grade and, in that grade, not one millimetre of loose gum vein is permitted. In an F17 structural grade the permitted amount is 1/6th of the length. This post would have started as a 1.5m so even then it should only be a maximum of 250 mm long. I imagine that I and other reputable suppliers priced this job and went to the builder with a price of say $30 per metre for in grade material. The builder would have taken one look and said, "You are too dear. I can purchase this for $25 per metre". It is a good deal for the miller as this piece should have gone down the chipper. Inspections for conformance to grade should be done more often.

2. Builder's care. Had the builder simply taken this piece and turned it 180 degrees and placed the split outwards, the visual effect would have been far different. He may not have understood what he was looking at, i.e. what an open gum vein is and it would not have looked as bad as this when installed, but pride in what you are building tells you that it will look a lot better if you place it away from view. It got so bad that I had to start putting labels on reversible products stating which side had to be placed away from view as I could not trust people to look discerningly at two sides.

3. Top Fixing. The screws fixing the rail to the post are just driven through the rail into the end grain of the post. Bad practice will always beat you. Moisture works its way down the screw holes and it just has to deteriorate. The only way to fasten a top rail sitting on top of a post is with brackets from underneath. The image on the right is from a boardwalk where the long run of top rail is fastened the way I recommend. Then one day someone added an approach railing and just fastened the top rail from the top. It did not work.

Fig. 136. Top fixing has failed.

4. Top rail is flat. By not allowing the top surface to shed moisture the timber deteriorates far more quickly. Either sloping the top rail or using a moisture shedding profiles would significantly improve the life of the rail without increasing the cost.

5. Termination of wires. Frequently, we see on the drawings some lines with an arrow saying "stainless wire rope". Perhaps a size and a spacing is mentioned but generally a specification that you can drive the proverbial bus through. This image is a good example of why firm direction has to be given. We built a bridge for a client to their drawings which terminated in eyed coachscrews. The post split and we were asked to fix it. We thought it was a design fault but we held our peace and fixed it. We later were asked to build another bridge with the same detail and so we asked for the detail to be changed. They would not and the post again split. We were asked again to fix it but this time refused to do it for free. Of course, we never got another job from that company.

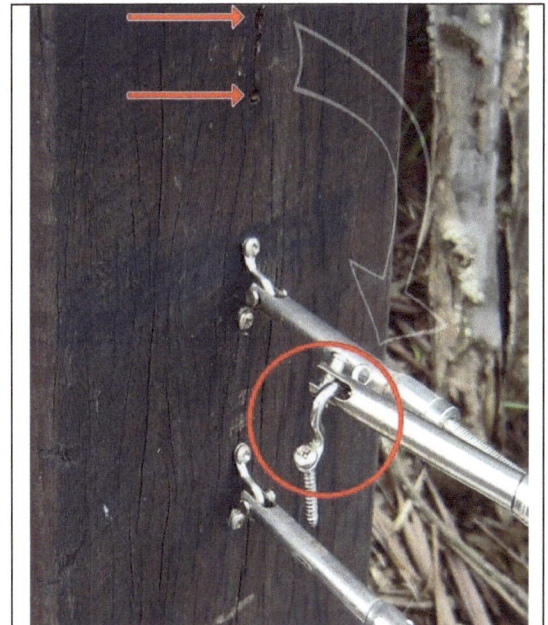

Fig. 137. Saddles have failed.

6. Film Forming Finish. You can see that moisture is getting under the film at the join in the top rail. This is going to promote degrade at the end grain. Also, when the film breaks down, and it does not take long in our high UV, you may have to sand the coating off before you can apply a new coat. For a full discussion on finishes refer to my book, *Architectural Timber Battens*.

There is not one issue in this case history that is difficult to understand and could not have been fixed on paper - including confirmation grading as part of the specification. I would have also added the use of a volute washer so the post would not have needed retightening.

11. Foundations

Frequently a footbridge is not considered in its entirety of a superstructure, fitted to a substructure and married in to a footpath. Instead it can be thought of simply as a superstructure so causing problems as other trades try and marry their work into the stand alone bridge.

You would not expect there to be a big difference in superstructure costs between kit bridge suppliers. You would anticipate that engineers applying the same code would come up with roughly similar steel sizes for the same application. Yet, strangely, I have observed that steel sizes vary drastically, particularly on trusses. But despite that, frequently the major cost difference between kit bridges is the installed price because of the vast differences in foundations.

Fig. 138. Hardwood Post set in concrete – less than 25 year design life.

Fig. 139. 50mm trip hazard after about 8 years on the same bridge.

General Considerations

It is possible to build a foundation that is very inexpensive but, should they be accepted? The hardwood post in Figure 138, even if it is In Ground Durability 1 would have a life expectancy of 25-50 years. This means a design life of 25 years. But that 25 year period is only if the post is set in natural earth, fine crushed rock or no fines concrete. The design life is shorter when set in concrete. How much shorter will all depend on how much it rains. My home locality, the Lockyer Valley, is one of the worst areas in Queensland for groundline decay so I am particularly conscious of this. I have seen an Ironbark pole rot of at ground line after 14 years simply because it was set in concrete. In the project shown in Figures 138 and 139, low cost foundations were chosen over concrete abutments where the approach path, over highly reactive soil, was tied into foundations to prevent differential movement between the bridge and the footpath. The consequential differential movement has resulted in a dangerous trip hazard. There are major public liability issues that can result if a holistic approach is not adopted.

The timber in the trussed bridge illustrated is pine treated to H3. After the soil has encroached on it (and really in any case where there is less than about 200mm clearance), it has become a H5 application. The Timberlife design life prediction software estimates the serviceability (50 % strength) of a 150x50 pine treated to H3 when used in an above ground application of somewhere between 75 to 90 years and replacement at about 100 years. When the same timber is in ground contact it only has a serviceability of 25 years. These examples show that a low initial cost for the foundations can be very expensive in the long run and it is therefore important not to accept them.

Fig. 140. No side walls allow soil to encroach on H3 treated timber.

Fig. 141. Well detailed abutment for a timber bridge.

Unless there is a very good reason why not, and they do occur, a specification for a footbridge should stipulate that the abutments are to be built in concrete and incorporate an integral back and side wall. Further features of a well designed foundation should include a sloping surface towards the front to shed any moisture, have the girders or bearings (when used) set about 25-50 mm above the foundation on dry pack[64] and allow for easy inspection for termites, rust etc.

Timber shrinks and this shrinkage has to be considered in the design of the abutments. Pine and hardwood in ex 50mm thick sizes can be purchased seasoned of course but, for many applications, they are just too light to be used for trusses. Fastener damage precludes their use as joists. So for many, if not most applications, you will be dealing with unseasoned timber. This is why it is important to have controlled the species used so you know how much shrinkage you have to design for. If you have just said something like F14 hardwood you could be dealing with anything between 6 to 13% shrinkage. On a 200 mm beam with 35 mm decking this means shrinkage could be between 14 to 30 mm if you have not taken control.

---

[64] Dry pack cement is formed with a ratio of 1 part of cement to 3 parts washed sand by weight mixed with 0.25% water to the total dry weight. Initially trowel mixture under the bridge bearings Ram the dry pack against a board using a hammer to compress the mix.

Fig. 142. Adjustable tread.

Fig. 143. Adjustable height hold down.

For boardwalks, we use 150 mm joists in spotted gum. Theoretical shrinkage with a 35 mm deck is 11 mm. Over a millimetre of shrinkage will have already taken place by the time the job is complete so it can be dealt with by setting the decking 5 mm high on completion and so, after seasoning, will be less than 5 mm under the approach meaning you have compliance with the trip hazard requirements of the disability code. But most bridges will require you to plan to compensate for much more. Figures 142 and 143 show two ways of doing this. The one has a tread that is adjustable for height and the other has a hold down system where the height can be adjusted.

Fig. 144. The path has settled.

There are times when the bridge is on very solid foundations but the approach path is on fill. There are various ways of joining the path to the bridge but what you do not do is ignore the risk. With the example shown in Figure 144, the bridge ended on a set of piles and the timber overhung and butted against a path at right angles to the bridge. The repair saw the timber planed down and an aluminium checkerplate then screwed over the join. While this particular case was repaired under the builders guarantee period, these trip hazards can be left unattended for years and, only be rectified after an accident. A set of piles could have been installed under the path prior to it being installed to support it as it passed by the bridge. No doubt the path would have cracked but, cracked concrete is preferable to a broken leg.

Piles and Piers

Fig. 145. Heritage listed railway bridge in Coominya, Queensland (built 1885)

Timber piles are unaffected by acidic or alkaline soils that would attack other materials and, that portion below the ground water line can have an almost indefinite life. This makes them the perfect carbon sink. In certain applications timber piles can outlast alternative materials. Examples that have been cited are the reconstruction in 1902 of the Campanile Tower in Venice on 1000 year old piles which were in perfect condition and the 600 year old piles under Old London Bridge.[65] Piles are vulnerable at groundline which is why foundations and piers often use concrete in this area. Figure 145 illustrates where the piles which would otherwise be subject to wetting and drying, terminate in a concrete plinth.[66] Where piles extend out of the ground the designer should consider the use of boron rods and a boron based pole wrap. Preservation works very well on natural round as there is a full band of treated sapwood around the heartwood but softrot and brownrot can still attack treated timber. In Queensland, powerpoles are inspected after 10 years service and every 5 years thereafter with a fresh pole bandage applied. This approach should be considered along with replacement of the boron rods.

---

[65] Freedman. *Timber...*, 47-8

[66] These piles are 20 m out of the ground. They were originally in the ground as well meaning these would have been approx. 25 metres long!

Crib Foundations

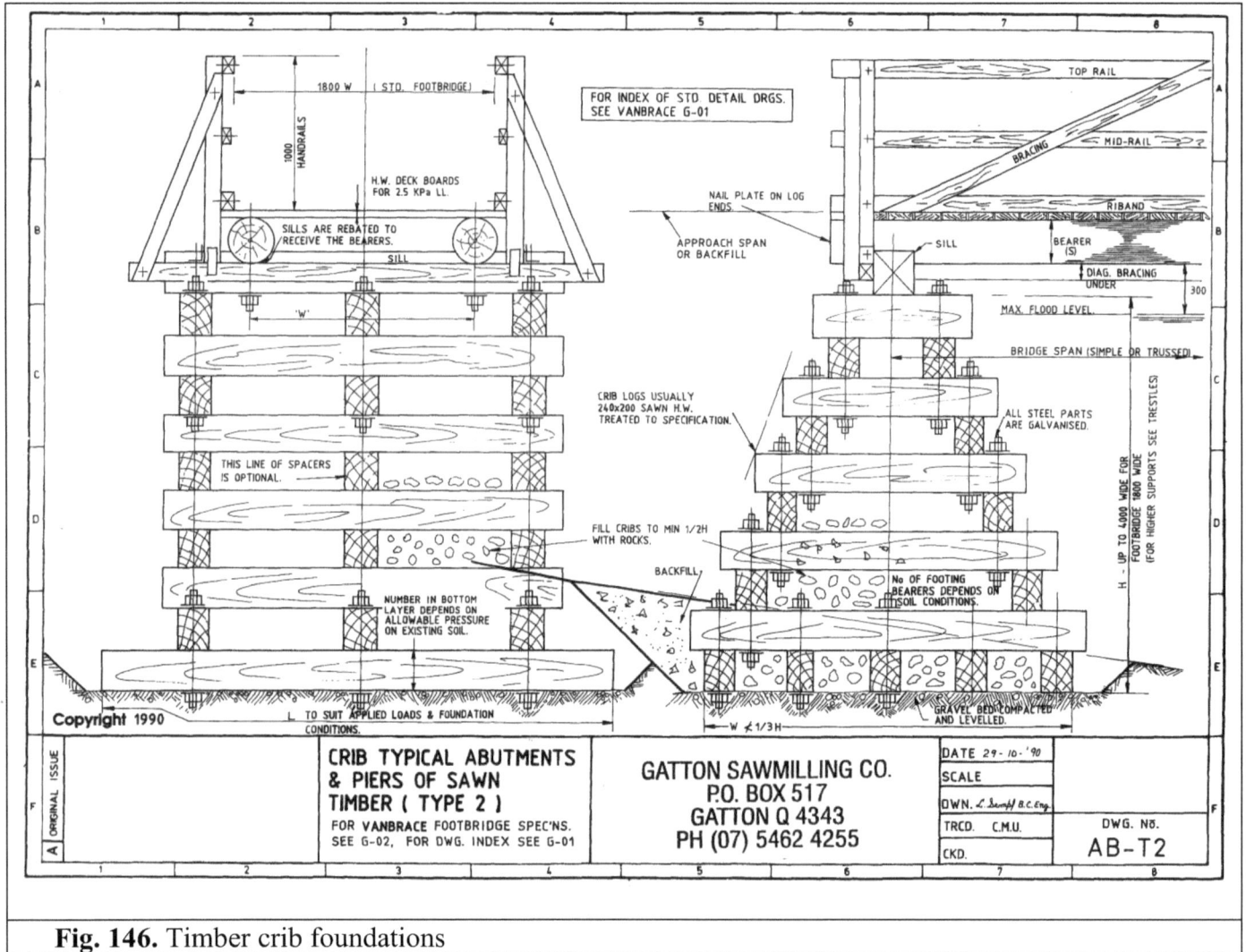

Fig. 146. Timber crib foundations

Timber cribs are a quick foundation with light components which makes them suitable for temporary work such as supporting a bridge while the abutment or pier is being repaired. Their low cost and relative durability can make them a foundation of choice in walking tracks where soils are unstable and subject to wetting as the weight is distributed over a broader footprint. Incised pine treated to H5 would be ideal but only H4 is probably available. This can be improved with a coat of CN Oil with CN emulsion where the timbers touch. When the crib is filled with rock it becomes very stable. In reality, not many designers will encounter an application where these will be the preferred answer. Shrinkage relative to the approach path is likely to be an issue.

12. The Tender Process

Before you Start

A client wanting a footbridge **MUST** be prepared to do basic preliminary work. A cross section of the waterway **must** be prepared and made available in CAD format. It should show the Q100 flood level and the normal stream level. A soil test must be taken and a recommendation given and a stream flow nominated. Our experience is that this is usually not done. The prevailing view with the soil test seems to be – let the contractor price this in to the project and we can get this tender out with minimal cost and outlay. But this is false economy. The tenderers are not going to undertake the investigation prior to quoting. Instead there will be assumptions made and these will assume worst case scenario and will result in estimating the cost of foundations that are generally more expensive than if the actual conditions are known. The asset owner, who has tried to save money, eventually, pays for the soil test plus the contractor's margin plus what is "pocketed" through the site being easier than assumed. Alternatively a quote may nominate its assumptions and a claim made if foundations requirements are outside of those nominated.

Not every bridge can be built above the Q100. When the bridge is likely to be inundated a design speed must be nominated. We once quoted a major bridge where the velocity was not nominated in the documentation. On phoning the client I was advised that I had to undertake our own flood study prior to quoting so "the Council did not have to bear any of the risk" as "Council does not have the resources or data available to provide tenderers with advice regarding velocities". Fortunately a very helpful engineer heard through a third party that we were floundering and advised that there already was a flood study in their office with all the information I needed. The bridge was 34 metres clear span and the flow was 2.9 m/s and had to be quoted as a truss! We could not provide an economic truss to meet that specification. Earlier advice was that the bridge was situated in a backwater and there was no flow.

Fig. 147. The deck of this timber bridge has dropped into the creek!!

The client has a very large investment in infrastructure both in dollars and in reputation, if a bridge fails, the public will see it as failure by the asset owner, not failure by the contractor. The first step in protecting the asset owner's reputation is through supplying full and accurate information at the design stage. It is also the first step in minimising the cost.

The reasons you should consider a tight specification are:

- To protect the public,
- To ensure public funds are spent well,
- To protect reputations,
- To protect non specialists purchasers/specifiers,
- To assist non specialist assessors; and,
- To provide a level playing field for suppliers

Site Survey[67]

A site survey is necessary as a design aid and to properly locate the structure within the landscape. This is necessary from an aesthetic and practical point of view as, generally, most bridges are not built on site but the superstructures are prefabricated. Suppliers do not have the luxury of building to fit the actual site - only the representation of the site - so the site plan must be as complete as possible so that the structure fits both the site and its landscape setting.

The first source of information may be an ortho-photo that often includes contours. A detailed contour survey extending 50m up and 50m downstream is usually the best way of presenting the information together with a survey of the possible connections to the pathways. This should also include top of bank, existing water levels, tidal range, observed tide, relationship to AHD or tidal datum. Debris marks, flood levels, evidence of soil scour or siltation are all important.

Obstacles should be located on this plan including services (underground and overhead), pits and valves, signs, property boundaries, trees (including type, girth and root buttressing), roads, paths, fences barriers etc. Sufficient recovery marks including temporary benchmarks should be installed at this stage to enable future set-out. This work is best done by engineering surveyors with the output direct to the software used by the engineer.

The hydraulic consultant may also need information on upstream properties that could be affected by any damming effect of construction. Information on heavy vehicle access for construction, storage areas and site. Photos are also required.

Geotechnical Investigation

Over the years we have been presented with some very strange reports, for example we have received reports suitable for a house slab and even one for a road. But the requirements for a bridge are very specific. Unless you can see rock, you have to assume it is highly probably you may have to use piles rather than a pad footing.

In comparison to typical civil engineering and building work, footbridge foundations are lightly loaded. Working bearing pressure on standard footings has been kept to 50kPa, acknowledging that the locations are often unsuitable for housing where 100 kPa is the 'norm'. Working loads on piles are typically less than 100 kN - an order of magnitude less than 'conventional' piling (1000 kN). This means that light plantation pine piles are frequently used, making for economies in handling and driving. Piles may not have to be driven to rock by using skin friction to carry most of the load.

While the ground loadings for typical footbridges are quite small, they still need to have adequate foundations. All bridges require a geotechnical investigation to determine the nature of the founding material so that economical foundations can be designed to adequately withstand the anticipated loadings.

Usually where we bridge creeks, the ground is poor, unconsolidated, erosion prone, waterlogged and susceptible to flooding during construction. In that situation small capacity driven timber piles are the foundation of choice. Where the ground is stronger (50kPa allowable bearing pressure or better), consolidated (will not compress with time), erosion resistant, and above the watertable, a strip footing is the preferred option.

---

[67] The comments on site survey and geotechnical investigation are from my Light Bridge Manual.

More sophisticated bridges like arches or suspension bridges impose considerable horizontal forces and so require good foundations. Simple bridges with small spans and free from inundation are the other end of the spectrum and are both versatile and adaptable.

The minimum geotechnical requirements are for a borehole at each abutment and pier position. In each bore SPT's (Standard Penetration Tests) or undisturbed tube samples should be taken at regular depth intervals as a means of establishing soil strength. These bores should be supervised by an appropriately qualified professional. Bore depths would typically be 2-4m deep on good 'residual soil' sites (strip footings) and 5-9m or deeper on 'soft soils' or 'alluvial sites' (driven piles). In cases where access for the drilling rig is limited, DCP's (Dynamic Cone Penetrometer) can be taken adjacent to the SPT and then at the other (hand augered) boreholes where the drilling rig cannot reach. SPT's are preferred as they are universally available and correlate better with driven pile resistance.

Make sure you get a recommendation!!

A suggested Specifications with a checklist are as follows:

FOOTBRIDGE SPECIFICATION & ASSESSMENT CRITERIA
Notes

This specification is NOT applicable for a

- bridge over a major road or railway
- bridge assessed as a Walking Track Structure (AS 2156.2)
- dedicated bikeway or shared use path (see separate Spec.)
- bridge with a deck area >85 m^2
- bridge with substantial tractor/mower loads

The bridge shall be designed in most respects to AS 5100 Bridge Design but with special attention drawn to the following conditions/variations

Condition	Requirements	Conform – circle which applies		
BASIC PERFORMANCE REQUIREMENTS				
Span at hold down bolts is		Yes	No	?
Clear width between handrails is		Yes	No	?
Distributed load	5 kPa	Yes	No	?
Point Load	4.5 kN	Yes	No	?
Load Factor (not over a road/railway)	1.5	Yes	No	?
First Natural Frequency	3.5 hertz	Yes	No	?
Note: A bridge of 3 kPa will not be accepted				
EXTRA REQUIREMENTS FOR SERVICE VEHICLE				
A service vehicle with a GVM ??? will also use the bridge at low speed	Yes or No	Yes	No	?
Minimum width requirement is 2.7m		Yes	No	?
Distributed load		Yes	No	?
Point load		Yes	No	?
INUNDATION				
This bridge will be submerged in a Q100 event	Yes or No	Yes	No	?
If *Yes*, what speed in m/s if not nominal	??m/s	Yes	No	?

The bridge will be submerged in what more frequent event	Q?	Yes	No	?
Design velocity if not nominal	? m/s	Yes	No	?
Flow height above deck		Yes	No	?
Flow depth to average stream bed		Yes	No	?
Shear restraints required when flooding is not nominal		Yes	No	?
HANDRAIL INFORMATION				
Minimum height	1.1m	Yes	No	?
To comply with BCA		Yes	No	?
To comply with AS 5100		Yes	No	?
Lateral Load	0.75 kN/m	Yes	No	?
Vertical Load	0.75 kN/m	Yes	No	?
Frangible Rails required	Yes or No	Yes	No	?
In other respects does the handrail comply with BCA	Yes or No	Yes	No	?
Stiffness required is span (between posts) of	1/800	Yes	No	?
Tamper resistant fittings to stainless wires?	Yes or No	Yes	No	?
Notation that horizontal rails are fixed from below	Yes or N/A	Yes	No	?
Notation that vertical rail screws are staggered	Yes or N/A	Yes	No	?
Note 1: with BCA compliant rails, any wires are 60mm apart at 2.0m post centres				
Note 3: Frangible rails must still meet 0.75 kN/m laterally and vertically				
MINIMUM STEEL THICKNESS				
4 mm for tubular sections		Yes	No	?
USE OF TIMBER				
Minimum grade for joists	F17	Yes	No	?
Acceptable species include Spotted Gum, Ironbark, Gympie Messmate. Blackbutt is not acceptable		Yes	No	?

Minimum grade for decking	F22 face	Yes	No	?
Acceptable species as per joists		Yes	No	?
Dampcourse is required on joists with CN emulsion		Yes	No	?
Decking to be Oiled with CN Oil		Yes	No	?
Rough sawn face specified for grip		Yes	No	?
Notation that deck screws are predrilled and staggered	Yes or N/A	Yes	No	?
Notation that joists are minimum 75 mm wide	Yes or N/A	Yes	No	?
Fasteners				
Are all fasteners to be stainless steel	Yes	Yes	No	?
NOTES ABOUT TRUSSES				
Note 1: Trusses are to be installed above the Q100 if forces more than nominal				
Note 2: Trusses shall be designed using the "U Frame' method				
Note 3: Balusters on truss handrail are to stand 100 mm free of the truss				
Note 4: "Duragal" is not accepted – hot dipped gal or high corrosion resistant paint only				
Note 5. Timber trusses are not to be nail plated unless closely screwed as well				
Note 6. If a paint finish is used for corrosion resistance is it at least equal to PPG's PSX700				
FOUNDATIONS				
Terminate with concrete abutments	Yes	Yes	No	?
Integrated side and back wall required	Yes	Yes	No	?
Is the approach path integrated into the abutment	Yes	Yes	No	?
50 year life on bridge bearings	Yes	Yes	No	?

DOCUMENTATION
At tender stage – typical drawings, images and/or brochures will suffice
On granting of order – Step 1 Assessment - working drawing prepared by a registered engineer marked "not for construction" are to be submitted for assessment. Plans are to be in English
On Granting of order – Step 2 – Approval – on assessment of drawings, and making any changed that are deemed necessary, a new set of drawings are to be submitted
On Completion of project – The successful tenderer *is/is not* (**delete whichever does not apply**) required to provide a certificate of construction

CYCLEWAY/SHARED PATH SPECIFICATION & ASSESSMENT CRITERIA
Notes
This specification is NOT applicable for a
- cycleway over a major road or railway
- bridge with a deck area >85 m^2
- bridge with substantial tractor/mower loads

The bridge shall be designed in most respects to AS 5100 Bridge Design but with special attention drawn to the following conditions/variations

Condition	Requirements	Conform – circle which applies		
BASIC PERFORMANCE REQUIREMENTS				
Span at hold down bolts is		Yes	No	?
Clear width between handrails is **(delete as needed)**		Yes	No	?
a. Commuting, Tidal flow, low use Minimum width	2.0m	Yes	No	?
b. Commuting and local access regular use - Minimum	2.5m	Yes	No	?
c. Commuting frequent and fast (30 kph) Minimum width	3.0m	Yes	No	?
d. Recreation regular use Minimum width	3.0m	Yes	No	?
d & c combined (30 kph) Minimum width	3.5m	Yes	No	?
Distributed load	5 kPa	Yes	No	?
Point Load	4.5 kN	Yes	No	?
Load Factor (not over a road/railway)	1.5	Yes	No	?
First Natural Frequency	3.5 hertz	Yes	No	?
Note: A bridge of 3 kPa will not be accepted				
EXTRA REQUIREMENTS FOR SERVICE VEHICLE				
A service vehicle with a GVM ??? will also use the bridge at low speed	Yes or No	Yes	No	?
Minimum width requirement is 2.7m		Yes	No	?
Distributed load		Yes	No	?

Point load		Yes	No	?
INUNDATION				
This bridge will be submerged in a Q100 event	Yes or No	Yes	No	?
If *Yes*, what speed in m/s if not nominal	??m/s	Yes	No	?
The bridge will be submerged in what more frequent event	Q?	Yes	No	?
Design velocity if not nominal	? m/s	Yes	No	?
Flow height above deck		Yes	No	?
Flow depth to average stream bed		Yes	No	?
Shear restraints required when flooding is not nominal		Yes	No	?
HANDRAIL INFORMATION				
Minimum height	1.3m	Yes	No	?
To comply with BCA		Yes	No	?
To comply with AS 5100		Yes	No	?
Second offset rail 150mm from main handrail required	Yes	Yes	No	?
Note: Barrier is required when the fall height is >250mm				
Lateral Load	0.75 kN/m	Yes	No	?
Vertical Load	0.75 kN/m	Yes	No	?
Frangible Rails required	Yes or No	Yes	No	?
In other respects does the handrail comply with BCA	Yes or No	Yes	No	?
Stiffness required is span (between posts) of	1/800	Yes	No	?
Tamper resistant fittings to stainless wires?	Yes or No	Yes	No	?
Notation that horizontal rails are fixed from below	Yes or N/A	Yes	No	?
Notation that vertical rail screws are staggered	Yes or N/A	Yes	No	?
Note 1: with BCA compliant rails, any wires are 60mm apart at 2.0m post centres				
Note 3: Frangible rails must still meet 0.75 kN/m laterally and vertically				

MINIMUM STEEL THICKNESS				
4 mm for tubular sections		Yes	No	?
USE OF TIMBER				
Minimum grade for joists	F17	Yes	No	?
Acceptable species include Spotted Gum, Ironbark, Gympie Messmate. Blackbutt is not acceptable		Yes	No	?
Minimum grade for decking	F22 face	Yes	No	?
Acceptable species as per joists		Yes	No	?
Dampcourse is required on joists with CN emulsion		Yes	No	?
Decking to be Oiled with CN Oil		Yes	No	?
Rough sawn face specified for grip		Yes	No	?
Notation that deck screws are predrilled and staggered	Yes or N/A	Yes	No	?
Notation that joists are minimum 75 mm wide	Yes or N/A	Yes	No	?
Fasteners				
Are all fasteners to be stainless steel	Yes	Yes	No	?
NOTES ABOUT TRUSSES				
Note 1: Trusses are to be installed above the Q100 if forces more than nominal				
Note 2: Trusses shall be designed using the "U Frame' method				
Note 3: Balusters on truss handrail are to stand 100 mm free of the truss				
Note 4: "Duragal" is not accepted – hot dipped gal or high corrosion resistant paint only				
Note 5. Timber trusses are not to be nail plated unless closely screwed as well				
Note 6. If a paint finish is used for corrosion resistance is it at least equal to PPG's PSX700				

FOUNDATIONS				
Terminate with concrete abutments	Yes	Yes	No	?
Integrated side and back wall required	Yes	Yes	No	?
Is the approach path integrated into the abutment	Yes	Yes	No	?
50 year life on bridge bearings	Yes	Yes	No	?
DOCUMENTATION				
At tender stage – typical drawings, images and/or brochures will suffice				
On granting of order – Step 1 Assessment - working drawing prepared by a registered engineer marked "not for construction" are to be submitted for assessment. Plans are to be in English				
On Granting of order – Step 2 – Approval – on assessment of drawings, and making any changed that are deemed necessary, a new set of drawings are to be submitted				
On Completion of project – The successful tenderer *is/is not* **(delete whichever does not apply)** required to provide a certificate of construction				

Appendix A – Deckling Specification

The following specification is used in conjunction with tapered sides and a profiled underside to produce Deckwood. Designers should not accept F14, or F17 with species mixes that include blackbutt. I have directly copied a specification from a large council that is written in such a way as to receive our Deckwood or a true equivalent for their bridges. Remember that Deckwood is not just a piece of timber, it is a whole system of building which this specification reflects.

1.00 Seasoned or Un-Seasoned?

Where timber planks are to be fixed directly to steel, Kiln Dried timber is required. This will be 136mm x 42mm F22 Top Un-Seasoned Grade or better Ex. 150 x 50 off saw. Where timber joists are incorporated so we can fix the planks to timber to timber 145mm x 45mm Un-Seasoned F22 Top Grade or better shall be used.

2.00 Fixings

For Timber to Steel use the Simpson Strong-Tie TBG Series to suit the plank and underlying steel joist thickness or similar approved by the Designer, BCW and CA For Timber to Timber use 14 gauge, type 17 with a countersunk/bugle head and a recessed hexagonal drive.

- All screws to be stainless steel, Grade 304.
- All screw holes to be pre-drilled with an appropriate bit combined with a countersink.
- Minimum screw length 75mm for 35 thick decking and 85mm for 45 thick.
- All deck fixings staggered with edge, end and spacings in accordance with AS1720
- Minimum Joist width 75mm.
- All bolts for Timber Joists etc to Structural Steel or Timber joist to Timber Bearer etc. to be minimum M12 316 Stainless Steel threaded rod with Glenlock nut and washer top and bottom.
- Timber joist tops should be coated with CN emulsion to counter the effects of water held at the joist-deck interface by capillary forces.
- In addition a Malthoid damp proof course (DPC) shall be laid along the joist-top protects the member from degrade. The Malthoid should be coated with a CN emulsion preservative paste to counter the effects of water held at the joist-deck interface by capillary forces.
- For steel joists Denso tape in place of the CN emulsion and Malthoid.

3.00 Species

Timber shall be selected from the following species:-
- spotted gum
- tallowwood
- ironbark.

4.00 Timber Quality

Timber will be graded under a hardwood quality control programme conforming to ISO 9002. At the time of grading, the bottom and sides of the plank will conform to AS 2082, Structural Grade No 2 while the exposed sawn (upper) face surface shall be free of:
- Loose and unsound knots
- Shakes
- Loose gum veins

- Knot holes
- Termite galleries
- Want, wane and bark
- Checks wider than 1mm
- End splits wider than 1mm
- Included bark
- Borer holes larger than 3mm diameter
- In addition, permitted defects will not cover more that 15% of the top face.
- Permissible defects on the upper face may include 1 only borer hole up to 6mm diameter per plank.

5.00 Preservative Treatment

Treatment, natural durability classes and combinations will conform to AS 1604, TUMA (Timber Utilization and Marketing Act Qld 1987) and TMA (Timber Marketing Act NSW 1977). Sapwood will be treated to Level H3 in accordance with TUMA. A certificate of treatment will be provided.

6.00 Tolerances

The actual cross-sectional dimensions of timber at the time of processing shall not vary from the dimensions stated by more that the following:

- width 3 mm
- thickness 0, +2 mm
- length 0 mm
- length (cut to size) 5 mm

Length	Maximum Bow	
	35mm	45mm
1800	10	10
2400	20	15
3600	50	35
4800	70	50

Length	Maximum spring(mm)			
	70 wide	90 wide	120 wide	145 wide
1800	7	5	4	3
2400	12	10	7	6
3600	25	20	15	13
4800	30	30	30	25

7.00 Surface Finish

Gauged on the bottom with the sound sawn face being exposed uppermost.

Timber to be coated with Lanotec, Tanacoat or similar subject to BCW confirming for CA approval the product's suitability after performance testing and establishing possible environmental impact, sustain ability and checking availability and lead times etc.

8.00 Laying

Lay the unseasoned timber edge face to edge face, and the kiln dried with a 3mm gap.

9.00 Contract

Allow 3 month lead time for Kiln Dried Timber

Appendix B. Use of Nailplates Externally.

pryda®

19th May 1998

Gatton Sawmilling Co.
P O Box 517
GATTON   QLD   4343

Attention: Mr Ted Stubbersfield

Dear Sir

Re Nailplates in external environment

I have your letter addressed to Chris asking for an opinion on the use of nailplates in external applications.

It is our experience that all nailplates in external use suffer from being squeezed out of the timber during repeated wetting and drying, especially if they also have direct exposure to the sun. We have observed nailplates being forced out by 2-3mm, and at this level of reduced embedment the load-carrying capacity falls by half.

This effect is more pronounced with softwoods than with hardwoods, and can happen even if the timber is painted.

Accordingly we recommend that nailplates not be used for structural purposes if they are to be exposed to the weather. In special circumstances, the nailplates can be prevented from being squeezed out by fixing screws (or threaded nails) at close centres all over the nailplate, but this is so labour intensive to be prohibitive unless there is absolutely no other option.

We do specify some types of nailplates for external use, such as in anti-split applications, but this is non-structural.

If the application is open to the environment, but otherwise protected against rain and sunshine, then the nailplates can be regarded as being in normal use, unless the environment is aggressive towards steel. In this case the nailplate needs additional corrosion protection. The same applies if the nailplates will be subject to salt deposition from a windy coastal environment.

Any further inquiry on this matter may be directed to myself on Chris's behalf.

Yours faithfully

Graham Cooper.

G J Cooper
Group Manager - Technical Development

cc Chris Rogers

Pryda (Aust) Pty. Ltd.
A.C.N. 006 630 137
Head Office: 29 Healey Road, Dandenong, Victoria, Australia 3175.
Tel: (03) 9706 5488 Office Fax: (03) 9706 5499 Sales Fax: (03) 9706 5496
Postal Address: Locked Bag 1407, Dandenong South, Victoria, Australia 3164.
Offices in: Sydney, Brisbane, Adelaide, Perth, Auckland, Napier, Christchurch,
Kuala Lumpur, Penang, Johor Baru, Bandung

Quality
Endorsed
Company

pryda solutions

Appendix C. Different Handrail Terminology

In Volume 2 of the Building Code of Australia, reference is made to "barriers" and "handrails" but, it is not immediately clear what the difference is and, the terms appears, at times, interchangeable.[68] There, a handrail may in some cases be a simple top rail or may comprise the complete assembly of top bottom and infill . What most laypeople would call the series of vertical balusters would be balustrades but in Volume 1 of the same document we find the whole assembly is called "balustrades".[69] If we look at the disability code there is only reference to "handrail" which can be a single supported rail or, at times, what others would call the grabrail used in conjunction with a barrier. Looking again at bridge code we have "pedestrian barriers" which are also called a "pedestrian railing".[70] A totally different term is used in Austroads' *Part 14 Guide to Traffic Engineering Practice - Bicycles* where a cycleway rail on a bridge is called a "fence".[71]

Looking further, the Walking Tracks standard has "barriers" which is any fence, handrail and balustrade.[72] This Standard does not define the individual components of the barrier. To add more diversity, Timber Queensland in their publications refers to handrail, bottom rail and balusters, all of which make up balustrade.[73] There the handrail would be different to a handrail to the disability code.

International readers have even more choice, TRADA in their publication on footbridges speak of parapets and handrail, intermediate rails, spindles and posts.

---

[68] NCC. 2015 Building Code of Australia – Volume 2. Part 3.9.2. 344-352.
[69] NCC 1014 Building Code of Australia – Volume 1 D2.16. 206-7.
[70] AS 5100.1 – 2004 12.1-3.
[71] Austroads. Part 14 Guide to Traffic Engineering Practice – Bicycles (Sydney: 1999) 115.
[72] AS 2156.2 1.5.2.
[73] Timber Queensland. *Technical Data Sheet 12*. June 2012, 1.

Source of Images

Images not mentioned are copyright to the author

2	Damaged bottom chord	James Pierce, James Pierce and Associates
6	Chapel Bridge, Lucerne	By Ikiwaner (Own work (Eigenes Bild)) [GFDL (http://www.gnu.org/copyleft/fdl.html) or CC-BY-SA-3.0 (http://creativecommons.org/ licenses/by-sa/3.0/)], via Wikimedia Commons
7	Sawmill Creek bridge	Government of New Brunswick
8	Pyrmont Bridge	"Pyrmont Bridge February 2014" by Nick-D – Own work. Licensed under CC BY-SA 3.0 via Commons – https://commons.wikimedia.org/ wiki/File:Pyrmont_Bridge_February_2014.jpg #/media/File:Pyrmont_Bridge_February_2014.jpg
9	Timber highway bridge	Dan Tingley, Wood Research and Development
12	Szechenyi Bridge	Monika Horvath, Raab Wood, Hungary
13	Japanese suspension bridge	Ken Thompson, Matrol Pty Ltd.
14	Cable Stayed bridge	Dennis Clark, Dennis Clark Photography
15	Aluminium truss	James Pierce, James Pierce and Associates
16	40 m bridge	Rod Bligh, Bligh Tanner
18	Covered bridge	"Baumgardener's Covered Bridge Inside Center 3008px" by Photo by and (c)2006 Derek Ramsey (Ram-Man) - Own work. Licensed under GFDL 1.2 via Commons - https://commons. wikimedia.org/wiki/File:Baumgardener%27s_ Covered_Bridge_inside_Center_3008px.jpg#/ media/File:Baumgardener%27s_Covered_Bridge_ Inside_Center_3008px.jpg
19	120 m truss	Dan Tingley, Wood Research and Development
24	Interior of Sawmill Creek	Dan Tingley, Wood Research and Development
27	Garo Garo	Timber Queensland
28	Empty Wood vessels	Gary Hopewell, DAF
29	Closed wood vessels	Gary Hopewell, DAF
32	Park Bridges	Dennis Clark, Dennis Clark Photography
36	Wrong engineering	Dennis Clark, Dennis Clark Photography
40	Bike wheel in decking	Murray Flemming, Canberra Outdoor Structures
44	51 year old bolt	Timber Queensland
49	Joist hangers on bridge	Jason Millard
54	Covered bridge, Sandgate	Dennis Clark, Dennis Clark Photography
55	Barrup truss bridge	Susan Stewart, Brisbane City Council
57	Main Roads Bridge	Dept of Transport and Main Roads
59	Horizontal Fixing	Dan Tingley, Wood Research and Development
61	Timber Truss on rounds	Dept of Transport and Main Roads
67	Maclean Bridge	Queensland State Archives ID 1763954 negative No. 438
68	Finke Truss	Queensland State Archives ID 1822602
69	Timber truss at Ravenshoe	State Library of Queensland

71	Railway truss bridge	Queensland Rail
75	Laminated beam	Dan Tingley, Wood Research and Development
84	Bridge delaminating	Dan Tingley, Wood Research and Development
85	Incised timber	Dan Tingley, Wood Research and Development
86	Delamination resistant beam	Dan Tingley, Wood Research and Development
87	120 m bridge	Dan Tingley, Wood Research and Development
91	Southgate Bridge rails	Grace Davies, Forest & Wood Products Australia
93	Swale drain	Dennis Clark, Dennis Clark Photography
94	Bikeway rails	Dennis Clark, Dennis Clark Photography
95	Combined rail	Dennis Clark, Dennis Clark Photography
106	Four handrails	Dennis Clark, Dennis Clark Photography
108	Queenslander rail	Dennis Clark, Dennis Clark Photography
109	Sandgate rails	Dennis Clark, Dennis Clark Photography
112	Moisture shedding rail	Dennis Clark, Dennis Clark Photography
114	Barrup truss	Dennis Clark, Dennis Clark Photography
120	Breaking line of sight	Dennis Clark, Dennis Clark Photography
121	Volute washer	Dennis Clark, Dennis Clark Photography
127	Warren truss timber rails	Dennis Clark, Dennis Clark Photography
128	Wires failing on barrier	Ronstan
130	Railings at Cairns	Ports North
137	Well detained abutment	Dennis Clark, Dennis Clark Photography
138	Adjustable tread	Dennis Clark, Dennis Clark Photography

Works Cited

Anonymous. *Dictionary Of Timber Terms* (Timber Secretarial Group: Sydney U.D.).

Austroads. *Part 14 Guide to Traffic Engineering Practice* – Bicycles (Sydney: 1999)

Australian Society for History of Engineering and Technology. *Timber Trussed Bridges of NSW.* URL: http://ashet.org.au/timber-truss-bridges/. Date visited. September 7, 2015.

Austroads. *Guide to traffic Engineering Practice*, (Sydney: Austroads 1999).

Francis, Lesley P and Jack Norton. Above-Ground Durability Estimation in Australia, Results after 16 Years Exposure, Document IRG/WP 05-20314. Paper given at the 36th Annual Conference of the International Research Group on Wood Protection, Bangalore. April 2005.

Freedman, G, C. Mattem. P. Larsen, S. Edwards, T, Reynolds. *Timber Bridges and Foundations. A Report Produced For The Forestry Commission*, November 2002. No publication details.

Government of New Brunswick. Transport and Infrastructure. http://www2.gnb.ca/content/gnb/en/departments/dti/bridges_ferries/content/covered_bridges/albert.html. Date accessed August 26, 2015.

Hyne. *Technical Data Sheet 6.* URL: http://www.hyne.com.au/downloads/technical_info/ TDS_6_MAY14_FINAL_WEB.pdf. Date visited. September 4 2015.

Lau, Benjamin. Repairs and Strengthening of Timber Bridge Trusses in *Proceedings of 1992 Timber Bridges Conference.*

NCC. 2015 Building Code of Australia – Volume 1 and 2,

Nguyen, Minh N, Robert H. Leicester, and Chi-hsiang Wang. *Embedded Corrosion of Fasteners in Exposed Timber Structures* (Forest and Wood Products Association: Melbourne 2008).

O'Connor, Colin. Bridging two centuries - *Historic bridges of Australia.* (St Lucia: University of Queensland Press 1985).

Pryda. *Technical Update Corrosion Resistance of Pryda Products* Feb. 2012.

Quensland Government *Twenty-sixth annual report of the Commissioner of Main Roads for year ended 30th June, 1947.*

Road and Traffic Authority. *Timber truss road bridges - A strategic approach to conservation, July 2011.* (New South Wales Government, July 2011). URL: http://www.rms.nsw.gov.au/ documents/projects/key-build-programs/maintenance/timber-truss-road-bridges/timber-truss-road-bridges-report-july11.pdf. date accessed. September 7, 2015.

Standards Australia. *AS 2156.2-2001 Walking Tracks – Infrastructure design.* (Sydney: Standards Australia).

Standards Australia. *AS 5100.1 – 2004 Bridge design - Scope and general principles.* (Sydney: Standards Australia).

Timber Queensland. *Technical Data Sheet 12.* June 2012.

Tingley, Dan. *Extending the Life of Hardwood Timber Bridges in Australia* a paper given at the 2014 conference of the Institute of Public works Engineering Australia, Queensland for Far North Queensland.

Thurman, E.G. Pyrmont Bridge – Construction & Restoration in Engineering Heritage Committee, Sydney Division, Institute of Engineers 1991. *Proposal to Landmark the Pyrmont Bridge, Darling harbour as a national Engineering landmark.* URL: https://www.engineersaustralia.org.au/portal/system/files/engineering-heritage-australia/nomination-title/Pyrmont_Bridge_Darling_Harbour_Nomination.pdf. 41.

.

.

Further Reading

Dennis, Ron. Footbridges. *A Manual for Construction at Community and District Level.* (International Labour Office: Geneva. 2004). Available at http://www.ilo.org/public/english/employment/recon/eiip/download/ratp/ratp11.pdf

Freedman, G, C. Mattem. P. Larsen, S. Edwards, T, Reynolds. *Timber Bridges and Foundations. A report produced for the Forestry Commission, November 2002.* No publication details. Available at http://www.forestry.gov.uk/pdf/intectbfrep.pdf/$FILE/intectbfrep.pdf.

Outdoor Structures Australia. *Deckwood Selection Guide.*

Outdoor Structures Australia. *Light Bridge Manual.*

Paths for All Partnership. *Path Bridges – planning design construction and maintenance.* No publication details available. Available at http://www.pathsforall.org.uk/satin/technical-information/bridges.html

Scottish Countryside Commission. *Footbridges in the Countryside.- design and construction.* (Perth: The Commission, 1981).

Stubbersfield, Edgar. *Architectural Timber battens.* (Gatton: Rachel Stubbersfield. 2015). Refer to chapter on hardware.

Stubbersfield, Edgar. *Deck and Boardwalk Design Essentials.* (Gatton: Rachel Stubbersfield. 2013). Refer to chapter on hardware.

Stubbersfield, Edgar. *Timber Preservation Guide.* (Gatton: Rachel Stubbersfield. 2012). Refer to section on treatment and corrosion.

About The Author

Ted Stubbersfield was born in the small Queensland town of Gatton in 1950. After studying to be a pastor in Brisbane and the UK he returned to the family business, Gatton Sawmilling Co. A fair question would be, "Can anything good come out of Gatton"? Well, Gatton was the home of a Governor General of Australia (William Vanneck 1938). It is also the home of the best and most innovative hardwood producer in Australia, Outdoor Structures Australia (OSA).

The family had been involved in sawmilling and building for about 140 years and a lot of knowledge has passed through the generations. In 1985 we ventured into the footbridge market (almost by accident) and then followed public landscaping. Initially, we just did as we were told by consultants who knew very little about timber. In about 1988 Ted decided he would come to know the medium he was working with far better than any of his competitors and most of the professionals who used his products.

Ted realised that there were no useful standards and guides for designing and building weather exposed timber structures such as boardwalks. That led in 1997 to his first formal research project on boardwalk design, engineering supply and construction. Over the years there followed a complete set of guides. These allowed professionals to design timber structures of exceptional beauty and durability. Typically, everybody wants to re-invent the wheel and the guides were usually ignored. Invariably, the same mistakes keep being made over and over. This little book is an attempt to remedy this.

In 2012, the time came to close the manufacturing arm of OSA and to take on a less stressful lifestyle. Ted plans to put in writing much of what he has learnt so the industry does not have to relearn it. This book on Timber Footbridges is the eighth in a series of Timber Design Files that are intended to show designers how to avoid the pitfalls of common, but often bad practice as well as Standards that can be very inadequate and engender a false sense of security.